The Unwritten History of Old St. Augustine

Also from Westphalia Press
westphaliapress.org

The Idea of the Digital University

Dialogue in the Roman-Greco World

The History of Photography

International or Local Ownership?: Security Sector Development in Post-Independent Kosovo

Lankes, His Woodcut Bookplates

Opportunity and Horatio Alger

The Role of Theory in Policy Analysis

The Little Confectioner

Non Profit Organizations and Disaster

The Idea of Neoliberalism: The Emperor Has Threadbare Contemporary Clothes

Social Satire and the Modern Novel

Ukraine vs. Russia: Revolution, Democracy and War: Selected Articles and Blogs, 2010-2016

James Martineau and Rebuilding Theology

A Strategy for Implementing the Reconciliation Process

Issues in Maritime Cyber Security

Understanding Art

Homeopathy

Fishing the Florida Keys

Iran: Who Is Really In Charge?

Contracting, Logistics, Reverse Logistics: The Project, Program and Portfolio Approach

The Thomas Starr King Dispute

Springfield: The Novel

Lariats and Lassos

Mr. Garfield of Ohio

The French Foreign Legion

War in Syria

Ongoing Issues in Georgian Policy and Public Administration

Growing Inequality: Bridging Complex Systems, Population Health and Health Disparities

Designing, Adapting, Strategizing in Online Education

Gunboat and Gun-runner

Pacific Hurtgen: The American Army in Northern Luzon, 1945

Natural Gas as an Instrument of Russian State Power

New Frontiers in Criminology

Feeding the Global South

The Unwritten History of Old St. Augustine

Copied from the Spanish Archives in Seville, Spain

by A. M. Brooks

Translated by Annie Averette

WESTPHALIA PRESS
An Imprint of Policy Studies Organization

The Unwritten History of Old St. Augustine,
Copied from the Spanish Archives in Seville, Spain
All Rights Reserved © 2017 by Policy Studies Organization

Westphalia Press
An imprint of Policy Studies Organization
1527 New Hampshire Ave., NW
Washington, D.C. 20036
info@ipsonet.org

ISBN-13: 978-1-63391-606-7
ISBN-10: 1-63391-606-5

Cover design by Jeffrey Barnes:
jbarnesbook.design

Daniel Gutierrez-Sandoval, Executive Director
PSO and Westphalia Press

Updated material and comments on this edition
can be found at the Westphalia Press website:
www.westphaliapress.org

Founding of St. Augustine By Pedro Menendez, September 8, 1565.

THE UNWRITTEN HISTORY of
Old St. Augustine

Copied from the Spanish Archives
in Seville, Spain, by Miss
A. M. Brooks and
Translated
by
Mrs. Annie Averette

PREFACE

We take pleasure in presenting to our readers information connected with St. Augustine never before published. It is composed largely of reports and letters to the King of Spain, much of it written by Pedro Menendez himself, and contains decrees and letters from the King to the Governor, Generals and Officers having charge of the Florida Provinces. It has been buried for over three centuries, in Seville, Spain. It is reliable, having been written in old Spanish and guarded with care. It contains facts for which many have sought in vain. The style in which it is written is clear and comprehensive, without being diffuse or overdrawn. It is the true history of our country.

CONTENTS

CHAPTER I—A. D. 1565........................ 1

Royal Decree from King Philip II in reference to further discovery and settlement of Florida—Officers and number of men appointed to go in the Armada—Reports from the Armada after leaving—Report from Pedro Menendez to his Majesty—The English and French have already settled here—Necessity of Spaniards taking entire control—Letter from the King to Pedro Menendez—Tells of English and French vessels reported to have sailed for these Provinces—King sends Fleet with sailors, soldiers and supplies that the person of Pedro Menendez may be guarded properly as Governor and Captain General of the Province of Florida.

CHAPTER II—A. D. 1565....................... 13

Pedro Menendez gives an account to his Majesty of the Fort Matanzas Massacre—Menendez and army escape from being made prisoners by the French on account of a tornado—Because of the swollen river the Council agree to make a land attack—Spaniards surprise and take Fort Matanzas without loss of a single man—Killing over two hundred Frenchmen and capturing Laudonnier—Find Indians enchanted with the Lutherans—Shipwrecked Frenchmen found on coast—With hands tied behind them are stabbed in the back by Spaniards.

CHAPTER III—A. D. 1598..................... 27

Report of Fernando Mirando, agent to the King, complains of Governor—Espionage over vessels—Gives account of work of negroes—Houses and churches built, land cleared—Soldiers assist in repairing Fort—Report of Bartolome De Arguellas—Capture of rebellious Indians—Sending some to Havana to be hanged, some to be imprisoned—Casiques render obedience to the Governor who assures them of his good intentions—Pedro Pertrene reports to the King of being newly appointed to be Captain of a Garrison in Florida—Insufficiency of salary to meet expenses—Because of long service to his Majesty implores aid and satisfaction — Dona Maria Menendez, Casique, writes the King asking aid in meeting the expenses of instructing the Indians in christianity and good government.

viii   *Contents*

CHAPTER IV—A. D. 1598...................... 34

Extract from official report made by Gonzales Menendez Canso, Governor and Captain-General—Six priests of the San Franciscan order murdered by Indians—Lieutenant Eciga sent to see if any of the priests are still living—Hears of one—Is refused permission to see him—After much persuasion and many threats Friar Fray Francisco is delivered—Manner of the death of the others is investigated—Fray Francisco makes a statement in regard to the death of the other priests, is forbidden by the Canons of the Church to reveal all—Notary Public Juan Ximanes swears to the investigation of several Indians through an interpreter—Execution of Indian Lucas as participating in the murder of Fray Blas.

CHAPTER V—A. D. 1600....................... 49

Letter from one of eleven monks sent out by his Majesty to spread the gospel—Report eighty churches in different Missions — Indians lazy and improvident — Avarice of Governor causes dissatisfaction—People desire his immediate removal—Fray Lopez, a Missionary, has converted many Indians in twelve years of service, among them Don Juan, a Casique, who stands highly among his people—His influence quells many uprisings—Juan Nunez Rios complains of Governor in a letter to the King—Begs for an open Port that the people may go back and forth and trade—An officer asks to be allowed to serve his Majesty elsewhere—Fray Blas DeMontes implores that he may be allowed to come to Spain for retirement—Gives account of a fire which burned the church among other houses—Slow progress among the Indians — Advices that a Bishop be sent—Report of Gonzales Menendez Canso to his Majesty—A shipmaster bearing dispatches shipwrecked in storm—Governor aids him from the Royal Treasury—Auditor from his Majesty arrives — Reports the Garrison abounding in fruits and grain—Grieves over the death of the Christian Indian Don Juan—Return of Fray Lopez from New Spain in good health—Reports the money brought to establish a hospital — More money needed for Garrison expenses—Francisco Redondo Villegas, Officer of Customs, is not treated with the respect due his Royal Office by the Governor—Reports affairs in a muddled condition—Soldiers well drilled—Much land under cultivation — Wages small — Rations insufficient.

CHAPTER VI—A. D. 1605-1608.................. 67

Minutes of a Bull or Bill of Supplication to be presented to the Holy See asking for concession of graces and powers for Catholic residents in Florida — Minorcan families brought priest and monk with them—Wish new privileges and graces granted—In regard to a Cedula from his Majesty, which instructs as to duties on wine—Priests and Monks of Tasco use Municipal monies for their own interests — Advises a change in the office of Treasurer of the Royal Chest—Vessels carry important papers for his Majesty lost — Favors shown to Don Francisco gratifies the people — Letter from Pedro Ibarra to his Majesty says there is not sufficient support for the Garrison—Solicits aid for a poor widow—Soldiers find amber in a fish, for which Menendez exacts a duty—French and English pirates cause much anxiety—A few captured, some imprisoned and ten hanged—Visiting Indian chiefs so impressed with the religious services and processions that they ask for friars to instruct their people—Asks for assistance in building a fort at the mouth of Miguel Moro—Endeavors to find the source of river San Mateo and Lake Miami—A garrison of warlike people—Proposition to establish a Manager of the Inquisition to subjugate and control them—Does not wish to let certain priest and captain—Report of Jaun Menendez Marquez—Deplores the decision to reduce the garrison—Advises a return to the policy of Pedro Menendez, his cousin—Desires permission to come to Spain to more fully lay the condition before his Majesty.

CHAPTER VII—A. D. 1622-1640................. 82

Report of Antonio Benavides to his Majesty—The Spanish King instructs the establishment of friendly relations with the English of the Carolinas—Don Francisco Menendez with other officers sent out—Mission fails owing to the English not having yet received instructions from London—Requested the removal of an English fort built on Spanish territory—Refusal—The matter fully laid before his Majesty—Report of Luis De Rojas—A Frigate sent out to assist a fleet in bringing supplies, run down by an enemy, boat stripped and burned, soldiers and crew escape to shore and finally reach the garrison—They collect Indians and soldiers and return—The enemy take to their launches and escape—Forty-seven persons only saved from a Spanish Fleet which had been captured by a Dutch Fleet—Recommends that his Majesty build a fort at the bar of the place called Jega—Report of Luis Ussitinez to his Majesty—The Mandate of the King carried out for prayer to Almighty God for the success of the King's arms taken up against France—At a meeting of the Board of the City Council of Havana appears a clergyman of the Holy Office of the Inquisition with an Auto from the Senor Commissionado, Don Francisco de las Casas, containing instructions as to certain ceremonies in connection with the Inquisition.

x   *Contents*

CHAPTER VIII—A. D. 1655-1657................. 96

An anonymous letter to his Majesty — Death of Governor Benito Ruid Salazer — Two others appointed to serve *pro tem*. die suddenly of a contagious disease — Certain related officials gather in the night and elect Don Pedro Ruitinez Governor — A distressing condition follows — The people's money squandered — Officials intimidated and abused — Material sent for repairing Fort used to barter with the Indians for amber and the money used by the Governor and Treasurer —Consults his own pleasure as to obedience to church laws and vows—A report from Diego Robelledo, 1657, as to the necessity of guarding the Ports of the Province owing to pirates and as a prevention from the enemy entering and entrenching themselves in some of the distant but rich Provinces—The Friars object to the fortifications as the Spaniards would retard the convertion of the Indians—The Governor thinks the real reason is, that because of the present condition the Friars are the masters of the Indians—A Friar reports to his Majesty that owing to the Governor insisting upon some Indian chiefs carrying heavy burdens of corn, when there were vassals for such labor — The chiefs cause an uprising — They march into the Garrison and hang the Governor—The Island of Jamaica heavily fortified by the English who intend taking Cuba, so it is rumored.

CHAPTER IX—A. D. 1662-1670.................. 107

Alonzo Aranqui y Cartez reports the auditing of accounts and condition of the Royal Treasury—Finding of large nuggets in a hill, supposed to be a silver mine—Goes to investigate— Report of Jaun Cebadillo to his Majesty of having sent out the King's orders concerning who shall keep the keys of the Royal chest — Administration of the negroes — Harshness shown the Royal employees—Francisco Guerra Vega reports a Captain of the Garrison for indecency and offense to his superiors, for which same he was reprimanded and imprisoned as a warning—Afterward given his liberty—The King to the Captain-General of Provinces of Florida—Instructions as to the continuance of the passage to Marcana Guale— Founding of the town of Santiago—As to the performance of certain duties by soldiers, for which money shall be paid— Soldiers shall be permitted to raise their crops, and not employed in personal work for the Governor—The Governor shall look after the wants and needs of his people—By order of the King, 1670.

CHAPTER X—A. D. 1671-1673.................... 112

Pedro Menendez received the title of Governor by right of conquest, and Captain-General and Commander of the Fleet

Contents

xi

by conference of his Majesty for faithful, valorous service—Don Martin Menendez receives the title of perpetual Governor by right of inheritance—Important papers burned at Simancas—Manuel De Mendoza reports to his Majesty as to the designs of the English enemy—Discovery of the South Sea—Condition of this Garrison and other Provinces—Implores aid in completing fortifications—Report to his Majesty by Francisco De La Guerre y Vega concerning an Englishman taken prisoner in the Province of Guale—One of a crew sent out from a settlement of English at St. Elena—This man who was second in authority was confined in prison on soldiers' rations—An effort made to break up the English settlement, which was unsuccessful.

CHAPTER XI—A. D. 1675...................... 121

Letters to the King from the Governor Pablo Ita Salazer—Oath of office administered in the tower of the old Fort which is rapidly going into ruins—The Garrison needing supplies and ammunition—No warehouses, and owing to the distance and frequency of storms delaying supplies, the people are forced to hunt in the woods for roots to appease their hunger—The Fort in danger from pirates—Ammunition and guards exposed to the fatalities of the weather—Pleads for more money to complete the Castle—Its great importance—A pentagonal shape recommended—The Viceroy of Spain fails to send the ten thousand dollars—One hundred men needed to guard the Castle—Great danger from pirates—Two hundred leagues from Havana and five hundred from New Spain.

CHAPTER XII—A. D. 1675...................... 130

An effort made to dislodge the English from Santa Elena—Governor ordered to complete the Castle and defense of the Garrison—Yucatan families—Master weavers asked for to settle in Florida—Appalache considered the best Province for settlement—Supplies sent from New Spain—Barracks to be made in the Fort for the soldiers—Money sent to finish the new Castle, also supplies for the soldiers—The neighbors to assist in building the new Castle—Repairs on the bulwarks of Guale—Increase of troops for St. Augustine—A fortress ordered built at Appalache.

CHAPTER XIII—A. D. 1680-1685................ 136

Letter from Pablo Ita Salazer to his Majesty—Indians of the Province of Guale declare themselves friendly to the English, and make war upon the Spaniards of the Island of St. Catherine—They surprise the six sentinels, killing all but one who escaped and gave warning—The people gather in the convent of a Friar and defend themselves from day light until four o'clock, when aid reaches them from the Garrison of St. Augustine, whereupon the enemy retires—The natives of the Island greatly alarmed—Disquieting news of the intentions of the enemy upon this Garrison—Implores aid from the King quickly, that the English may be ejected from the land—Don Jaun Marquez Cabera, Governor and Captain-General of Florida — Gives account to his Majesty of hostilities in the Provinces—Two Fleets, French and English, going and coming from Havana—Seize Fort Matanzas and, after plundering, burn it to the ground—Is now being rebuilt—Great depredations committed up and down the coast by the enemy—Pushing the work on the Castle—Grieved over its slow progress, owing to lack of workmen—Begs to be allowed to retire because of age and long service—To Charles II, our principal Casique, the King—From the people of the territory of Habalache—The King to the Governor and Captain-General of Florida—Concerning ten negroes from St. George, who asked for the water of baptism—A Sergeant-Major from St. George comes to claim them — Because they have become Christians the Spanish King decides to buy them—After receiving a receipt they are to be set at liberty, each one given a document to that effect—The King reprimands Don Diego Quiraga for not attending to these matters—Orders a full account to be sent as soon as it is accomplished.

CHAPTER XIV—A. D. 1689-1698.................. 147

Letter of the Governor and Captain-General of Florida, Don-Diego Quiroba y Losada, to his Majesty—Giving an account of a custom obtaining in the Garrison which endangers the safety of the people—When the Host is taken out in the night to administer communion to the dying the bells are rung until its return which is often hours, thus preventing the hearing the firing of the sentries across the river who are instructed to fire as often as there are numbers of vessels sighted—This danger fully laid before the Priest, who refused to discontinue the ringing of the bells, notwithstanding the city has been in arms awaiting the enemy for some days—In a Cedula by his Majesty of July 18th, 1674, he asks for a statement concerning the order and place of the Holy Tribunal of the Inquisition—These questions answered by Severino Mausaneda March 17th, 1690—An account of a military review in St. Augustine by Governor Don Diego Guiroga y Losada—Also recounts the great advantage to the City by building a sea wall to extend from the Fort the entire length of the City thus securing it against the sea which at present comes up to the houses during a storm—The soldiers and citizens subscribe ten thousand dollars, and the King is petitioned for aid that the citizens seeing his Majesty's interest will be encouraged to proceed—The King rebukes Governor Don Diego

Contents xiii

Guiroga y Losada of the city of St. Augustine for unjustly taxing the Indians—Misappropriating funds sent by agreement for canvas and provisions for them—Not attending to their wants and comfort and treating them alone as vassals—Extracts from the investigations of the Council as to alleged excesses committed by the Governor Don Francisco Moral Sanchez—His illtreatment of a Captain of Grenadiers—Acting according to his own will and not to military law—The Governor's removal desired—A report according to the King's command concerning affairs under Governor Don Francisco Morales Sanchez—Investigation shows that the facts set forth in the different papers and petitions sent to his Majesty to have been only too true—Impossible to put upon paper the strange, divers and extraordinary excesses committed by this Governor—The abuses sufficient to chill the soul and congeal the blood.

CHAPTER XV—A. D. 1708-1723.................. 163

Francisco Carcoles y Martinez in a letter to his Majesty reports all possible measures taken to prevent the destroying of this Province—Indians from the villages bordering on the Carolinas, aided by the English, each day carry off certain families, Christians and natives, more than ten thousand having been carried off to date—Probably sold into slavery—A Treaty urged with the English of the Carolinas, else there will be a continuance of hostilities and the spread of the Gospel impeded—In a second letter the Governor gives an account of certain Friars in a dispute with the Priest of the Parish concerning the rights to marry soldiers, Spaniards, Indians and half-breeds—The matter laid before the Governor, who in turn refers it to his Majesty—Recommends the abolishing of all Heathen customs—By a Royal dispatch, A. D. 1721, the Governor of Florida is commanded to go in person to the Governor of the Carolinas and arrange with him a Treaty of Peace between the English and Spanish of those Provinces adjoining—Which same was carried out as far as possible—Trinkets and clothing sent to the Casiques and chiefs of Appalachicola as commanded—Indians restless making preparations for war—English spreading dissatisfaction—A Council of war decides to send a vessel to Havana to the Governor asking for men, arms and provisions.

CHAPTER XVI—A. D. 1736-1739................ 174

Governor Senor Montiano in a letter to his Majesty says: It is reported that Don Diego Oglethorpe has said openly "that should he receive orders from his Government to fix the boundary lines between the Spanish possessions and the Carolinas, he would so delay its execution that there should never be a sign of these limits"—Montiano thinks "it will be impossible to ever discuss matters of importance with such a man and it will be best that he be removed"—An Indian, Juan Ygnacio de las Reyes, gives himself up to the English, under pretext of having killed an Indian, to gain information concerning the strength and intentions of the English toward the Spanish—After misleading the English as to the strength and numbers in the Spanish fortifications, he makes his escape and returns to this Province—Statement of what has been ordered for the aid of Florida Provinces—The dislodging of the enemy from certain settlements on its territory up to 1674 —Dispatch of 1675 commands that if the negro slaves sent to Havana have not already been sold, they shall be sent to Florida to be put to work upon the construction of the Castle to relieve the Indians.

CHAPTER XVII—A. D. 1741-1743.............. 185

A letter from the Governor Francisco Carcales y Martinez—Conduct of the Christians worse than the Heathen—Soldiers guarded while cutting timber to repair the Fort—The Castle in a tumble-down condition—The Garrison to be maintained for the propagation of the Holy Gospel and to shelter the workers of the Apostolic faith—A paper of representation to his Majesty concerning certain properties willed to the Royal Treasury by Don Francisco Menendez, and designated by the King for use as hospitals—The Royal Officers of the Province think these properties should be sold at auction, and the proceeds applied to the back pay of soldiers who are suffering and in need.

CHAPTER XVIII—A. D. 1770-1771.............. 191

A letter of resolution to his Majesty concerning a letter of appeal made to the Governor and Bishop of Havana asking for patent and Holy oil to administer baptism and extreme unction to the Catholic families taken from the Island of Minorca by the English—These families bringing with them Don Pedro Campos, Doctor of Sacred Theology, as a Parish Priest, and Don Bartolome Casanovas of the St. Augustine order as Vicar—These same claiming to have received their appointment from the Supreme Pontificate, not knowing to which Bishop the jurisdiction of Florida belonged—In order that a thorough investigation may be made the whole matter was referred to his Majesty—Letter of the Archbishop of Valencia concerning this matter—Letter of the Bishop of Cuba to his Majesty, expressing gratification over the zeal of his Majesty in this matter—Advices that the privileges be conferred—Letter of the Bishop of Minorca giving information concerning same.

Contents

CHAPTER XIX—A. D. 1771.................... 204

The opinion of the Judge—Having examined the different letters from the Bishop and made a thorough investigation into the matter concerning the granting of certain privileges to these Priests of the Minorcan families of the English colony of Florida, decides that these privileges should be granted as per reasons set forth in his written opinion, Madrid, 1771—Bishop of Cuba for the Council to Dr. Don Pedro Campos and the Rev. Father Bartolome Casanova, extending to these same Priests the title of Parish Priest and Vicar—Also sending a box containing three flasks of sacred oil—Hopes soon to be able to send a more extended prorogation of other powers — King solicited these powers from the Court of Rome—Asks for a detailed report of the number of families and condition of the congregation.

CHAPTER XX—A. D. 1773..................... 214

Proceedings of the Council at the Court of Rome concerning the appeal made by the Parish Priest and Vicar of the Catholic families established in the English colony of Florida—The different Bishops' letters—Also those of the Priest and Vicar asking for patent and further privileges and containing a report of the condition of the said Minorcan families who are dissatisfied with the lack of spiritual comforts—A brick church, and are very devout—Of their desire to throw off the yoke of Great Britain and their love for Spain—Reply of the Judge—Testimony sent by the Bishop of Cuba.

CHAPTER XXI—A. D. 1773-1786................ 226

Letter from the King to the Bishop of Cuba concerning the petition soliciting an extension of time and of the privileges for the Priest and Vicar of the Minorcan families in Florida, and enclosing an open mandate of His Holiness, enlarging and extending the time for twenty years—A copy of a letter and statement sent in by Lieutenant Don Nicolas Grenier in regard to the importance of the Provinces of the St. Marys and St. Johns rivers—The need of vessels to impress and control the inhabitants—Provinces rich in timber, turpentine, tar and pitch—Considers it detrimental to Spanish interests for Americans to introduce any commerce in the Provinces—Letter from the same Don Nicolas Grenier to the Governor urging the necessity of further protecting Spanish interests along the St. Marys and St. Johns rivers—Tranquility of the country jeopardized by outlaws—Some have been arrested and paid the penalty with their lives—Matter referred to the Governor—1774.

The Unwritten History
of Old St. Augustine

CHAPTER I.

A. D. 1565.

Royal Decree of King Philip II in regard to the further discovery and settlement of Florida—Officers appointed—Number of men to go in the Armada—Captains and men to be paid in advance, to increase diligence in service—Reports from the Armada after leaving — Pedro Menendez reports that the English and French have already settled here — Necessity of the Spaniards taking entire control of the country—Letter from the King to Pedro Menendez in regard to English and French settlers.

ROYAL DECREE.

THE KING.

To our officers who reside in the City of Sevilla in charge of the India contracts:

I have named the captains, as you will see, from the description shown by General Eraso, that they may enlist the 1400 men who are to go to Florida in the Armada which we have ordered equipped, instructing them immediately upon their arrival what they are to do, and notify me of their safe arrival. You must be immediately notified when the men are gathered together, and as it is expedient with each captain, you are to send a responsible person that he may pay each man one month's salary in advance from the treasury on the day he enlists. It will cost, we suppose, upwards of 11,000 ducats, that they may go provided according to instructions received. You are to give each captain a copy of the order sent, that he may be sure of his men—who, receiving this aid, neither he nor they be deceived. I also command that according to these orders you instruct the paymasters so that they may well understand that each soldier is to have the money in his own hands so that there be a good understanding between us. This is paid to them as it will be a long and arduous campaign, and so that they may work with more zest and the town be established quickly. See that the captains go at this work with diligence and haste, and you must immediately see and attend to where you are to lodge these people and from there embark them. Send with them a person of trust to guide and lodge them and to see that they are well provided with food and all necessaries for their money. Keep them well together without disorder or vexation to the people of the land. Inform me of how you have provided for them and you will have served me. From   BOSQUE DE SEGOVIA.

August 15th, 1565.

REPORT OF DON TRISTAN DE LUNA Y AVELLANO, CONCERNING AFFAIRS IN FLORIDA.

The Armada which went to found the town in Florida at the place called Santa Elena in the port of Juan Ponce on the eleventh of June, and sailed with good

Old St. Augustine

and mild wind. On the seventh day out we were on the river Espiritu Santo, twenty leagues south of said river, in 27th degree, from there we sailed six days to the southeast and south until we found ourselves in the chain. South from there we sailed north in search of the coast of Florida, and at the end of the eighth day, which was the eve of the visitation of Saint Elizabeth, we discovered the coast of Florida eight leagues to the west where the Armada cast anchor and took on water and wood. Now we began to have rough weather. From there the fleet sailed on the eighth of July in search of the Port Achusa, sending ahead along the coast a frigate, the pilot not knowing exactly where Port Achusa was. The Armada passed ahead and anchored in the Bay of Phillipina, which was discovered by Julio de Labazares, from whence the Governor sent to seek Port Achusa, having heard that it was the best and safest port on all that coast. Navigating along the same coast where the Armada had come, they found Port Achusa which is twenty leagues from Bay Phillipina and thirty, more or less, from the Bay of Miruelo, so that it is between two bays—latitude 30 1-3 degrees. On the return of the frigate with the news, we immediately determined to set sail with the Armada. It seemed best to have the horses go by land, so we put them off in said Bay of Phillipina, thus some of our captains made the trip overland with one hundred and forty horses, out of the two hundred and forty we started with, the others having died at sea. On the bar of Phillipina we had some trouble with the Armada in crossing, on account of its shallowness for the larger vessels, also the strong and swift current—besides the weather had changed, and it was rougher. The Armada left Bay Phillipina for Achusa on the 10th of August, the day of St. Lawrence, and it entered Port Achusa on the day of Our Lady of August, for which reason we gave it the name of St. Mary of Phillipina. It is the best port discovered in the Indias. The shallowest part at the entrance is eleven cubits, and after you enter there are seven or eight fathoms. It is spacious, having a front of three leagues, the Spaniards are already there. The entrance of the bar is half a league in width, on the eastern coast is a cliff at the mouth of the bay, and large vessels can anchor in four or five fathoms within a stone's throw from land. It is so safe that the winds and storms cannot hurt one. We found a few Indian ranches, they seemed to be fishermen. Judging from appearances it seems to be a fertile and good soil. There are many walnuts and many fruit trees—good hunting and fishing and good in many ways. We also found some plantings of corn. On the 25th of said month of August, the Governor sent Don Tristan de Avellano in a galleon, of those we brought, for this, from New Spain, with the news of all that had happened so far. He entered the Port of San Juan de Ulloa on the 9th of September. He will supply himself quickly with provisions, which at present we have sent to ask for, and we expect the boats to return soon. They will again go to this New Spain, and wait there to see the lay of the land, and where we are to found this town, and understand all the particulars and qualities to inform you.

When the boats return I will give the details to your Majesty in the order that the Governor, Friars and other Officers write me, and I shall be careful to aid them in the name of your Majesty with everything that they need, so they many not vex the natives, but give themselves up to friendly intercourse with them, until the time for planting grain. In future it will not be so expensive, the ground being so fertile we can gather large harvests, thus serving and exalting your Majesty and the Catholic faith of Our Lord.

To His Catholic Royal Majesty Pedro Menendez says:

That what he sends your Majesty is what he declares to know of the coast and lands of Florida, and of the corsairs whom it is said have gone to populate it and seize the vessels coming from the Indias—and the damage they may do, and the remedy to be used in cases where they should have settled. Give them no quarter, and appropriate the coast and lands so that they can be the more easily turned out—that your Majesty can send to spread the Gospel, prevent the damages that can be done the vessels coming from the Indias is as follows: That while in Sevilla last May, he knew and understood positively from persons coming from the Canary Islands that they had been on the Island of Teneriffe and Port Garachico with a Portuguese named Mimoso, who is a pilot on the run of the Indias, and has a wife and home in France, that he has become a pirate, seizing the vessels of your Majesty. He carried four men of war, and it was said he was going to settle the coast of Florida; that two other large vessels were awaiting him, as soon as he took on water and provisions in that port, and he saw them there in a small vessel without disembarking for five or six hours, where some of the people who wish to be under them came to speak to them. He then returned to his vessel and set sail to return to the Indias. Also, that he heard in Sevilla and in this court of your Majesty that the English had gone out with a fleet to the coast of Florida to settle and to await the vessels from the Indias—and about a month ago he learned that five large English galleons with heavy artillery had passed about the end of December along the coast of Gaul and the tempest had driven them into the harbor of Ferrol, where they were anchored for a day and a half without landing, but the fishermen had gone on board to speak to them. and he says: If the above be true, and the English, French or any other nation should feel disposed to go and settle any part of Florida, it would be very damaging to these kingdoms, because on said coast of Florida and in said strait of the Bahamas, they could settle and fortify themselves in such a way, that they could have galleons and vessels of war to capture the fleets and other private vessels that came from the Indias, and pass through there, as they would run great risk of being captured.

Also, that if last summer the French and English went to Florida as we are certain they did, and should have settled and built a fort in any port, and summered there, giving notice to their home government as to how they are situated, and should they be supplied this summer before we can raid upon them, and turn them out, it would be very difficult to do so on account of the friendship formed by them with the natives who would help them in such a way as to cause serious difficulty, and even should we finally succeed the natives would remain our enemies, and this would be extremely disadvantageous. Should they be supplied this summer the merchantmen which we expect from the Indias would also run great risk of being captured. Also, that it would be very annoying to have the above mentioned or others settle in Florida. Considering the proximity of the Islands of Santo Domingo, Puerto Rico and Cuba, where there are such vast numbers of negroes and mulattoes of bad disposition, there being in each of these islands more than thirty negroes to each Christian. And it is a land in which this generation multiplies with great rapidity. In the power of the French and English, all these slaves would be freed, and to enjoy their freedom would help them even against their own masters and lords and there would be an uprising in the land, and with the help of the negroes it would be easy to capture us. As an example of this, take Jaques de Soria, France, which in the year fifty-three, with one boat of a hundred tons and eighty men, by simply freeing the negroes, took and plundered the Islands of Margarite and Saint Martha, and burned Carthagena, plundered Santiago de Cuba and Havana, although at the time there were two hundred Spaniards there. They took the Fort with all it contained, and twelve pieces of bronze artillery and carried them all off. I consider these negroes a great obstacle to having the French or English settle in Florida or to have them so near, even though they should not be in favor with these two nations, there is danger of an uprising as there are so many cunning and sagacious ones who desire this liberty that I feel sure the design of those who should settle in Florida is to domineer over those islands, and stop the navigation with the Indias, which they can easily do by settling in said Florida. Also he says: That on account of these dangers and many others, it seems to him it would be to the service of God Our Lord, and your Majesty for the general good of your Kingdoms the Indies it would be well for your Majesty to try and domineer over these lands and coasts, which on account of their position, if other nations should go on settling and making friends with the Indians, it would be difficult to conquer them, especially if settled by French and English Lutherans, as they and the Indians having about the same laws, they would be friendly, and being near could rule and each year send out a thousand vessels to easily treat and contract with these lands which are said to be fertile and prolific for sugar plantations, which they so much need and are supplied from these Kingdoms. There might also be many cattle good for their tallow and wool and other necessities. What seems to him that your Majesty should do in the service of God and your Majesty's and for the salvation of so many souls, and the aggrandizement of your kingdoms and your royal estates, is as follows:

As there are neither French nor English nor any other nation to disturb them, that your Majesty should send five hundred persons, sailors, laborers, etc., and that among them should be one hundred master carpenters, blacksmiths, plasterers and builders of mud walls, all with their implements and appurtenances for every thing, with their arms of defense, such as arquebuses, cross-bows, etc. That among this number of five hundred people should be four Friars, four teachers and twelve Christian children, so that the principal Indians would send their children to school to learn to read and learn the doctrine of Christianity. There should be three surgeons who would go about in small boats, canoes or row boats with supplies for one year—go straight to Santa Elena and from there find all the paths, rivers and ports most suited and best, by land and water. See the condition of the land for planting and settle two or three towns in the best vicinity, build their fort, to be able to defend themselves against the Indians, that each of these forts should have artillery and ammunition. All this supply with the cost of the voyage will amount to eighty thousand ducats or more. There will be left vessels enough to carry a number of cattle. These must be sent from Spain, because in the Indias we could not find suitable vessels nor head workmen of the necessary qualifications and it could not give the desired results, besides the delay would cause much damage. It would be difficult to find the proper kind of people, and even if found the cost would be very much greater, as head workmen gain very large wages in those parts, as do also laborers and sailors. From Havana it would be still more impossible to bring them, as there are none to be obtained, and if they have to settle they must go a long way 'round, as they cannot enter the mouth of the Bahama Channel, it being as easy and quick to come from Spain as from Havana. It would be more important that your Majesty do this at your own cost and as briefly and with as secret a diligence as possible, and if your Majesty is not well served in this, find some one in whom your Majesty can place more confidence, confer with them and let them take charge of affairs—

although it would be far better for your Majesty to do this at your own cost, and with all brevity and secrecy which is the most important thing. Also, he says: That should there be French in this land or on the sea awaiting the merchant vessels from the Indias, it would be necessary to increase this squadron to four more galleons and one thousand men, principally marines—the cost of which for six months would be five hundred thousand ducats more or less.

PEDRO MENENDEZ.

THE KING.

To Gen. Pedro Menendez de Avilez, Knight of the Order of Santiago, and our Governor of the Province of Florida:

Know—Having understood that from the Kingdoms of France and England many war vessels have been sent out with a great number of sailors and soldiers, with intent of going to that Province, and that now again they are arming and equipping vessels for the same purpose at Havre de Grace and other Ports of said Kingdoms of France and England. And that you may do everything to defend yourselves and capture the Forts they have built and thrust them from the land, that you may hold it in peace. You might overlook the damage they have done to navigation. We have arranged for and ordered 1,500 infantrymen to join you and those you have with you and we send them with the fleet and also all the necessaries—and we have provided as Captain-General of the fleet Captain Sancho de Archimiaga, an expert and experienced man of the sea, ordering him to go to said Province, and in joining you, it gives you protection by sea as well as by land. Your flag alone must float, as our Captain-General, and all undertakings must be done under your flag. And for all enterprises to be undertaken by land we have appointed a Field Marshal and five Captains to be under him, and that both they and the infantry are to be directly under you as our Captain-General and Governor, because this is our will, and we have expressly ordered it. That your person must be carefully guarded. With your experience both by land and sea we are perfectly satisfied, still, that you may the better succeed, and that there may be conformity and good will, as it is important, affairs that between you and said Captain Archimiaga and Field Marshal and the other Captains accompanying him as they are men of much experience in war. It is our will, and so we order you, that in all things occurring on sea as well as on land concerning the war, you will call these Captains and consult with them, more especially Captain Archemiaga and the Field Marshal—that in this way alone must you decide upon questions of war—because thus it suits us and our service. That I trust in them to look into matters and provide all that is deemed advisable in such undertakings—and they will follow and obey you as our Captain-General. Let it be in such a way that there be good will and intelligence between you— no dissensions or quarrels, which would be a great drawback, but that you will proceed with mildness and consideration, as I feel assured you will, proceeding to free those lands, and give no quarters to the enemy to take root in them—and if it were possible, and there should be no notable inconvenience, you divide the fleet. Captain Juan Zurita and his company of

Artillery go with the Infantry, as you will see. Of their success you will see to it, and give an account.

PHILIP II.

Madrid, September 8th, 1565.

CHAPTER II.

A. D. 1565.

Menendez reports that his army escapes from being made prisoners by the French on account of a tornado—The Council agree to make a land attack, the river being too much swollen for their transports—The Spaniards surprise and take Fort Matanzas without the loss of a single man, killing over two hundred Frenchmen and capturing Laudonnier—The Indians enchanted with the Lutherans— Shipwrecked Frenchmen found on the coast—With their hands tied behind them they are stabbed in the back by the Spaniards.

FORT MATANZAS MASSACRE, 1565.

I wrote to your Majesty from aboard the galleon San Salvador on September 11th, this being the day she left Port. The duplicate of the letter goes in this, and later on will send the other. While I was on the Bar in a sloop with two small boats with artillery and ammunition there came upon us four French galleons which had run us down with two or three small vessels to prevent us from landing here. Taking the artillery and provisions, although the weather was not propitious for crossing the Bar, I preferred to take the chances rather than surrender myself and one hundred and fifty persons, who were with me, into their power. Our Lord miraculously saved us. The tide was low, there being only one and a half scant fathoms of water on the bar, and their vessel required one and a half long fathoms. They saw we had escaped them, as they spoke asking me to surrender, to have no fear. They then turned to search for the galleon, thinking we could not escape them. Two days out a heavy storm and tornado overtook them. It seemed to me they could not return to their Fort, running too great a risk of being lost, and to return to capture us they would have to bring a larger force and of the best they had. Thinking that their Fort would remain weak and it was the right time to capture it I called a council of the captains, who agreed with me, and decided to attack the fort by land. I therefore took five hundred men, the three hundred arquebusiers. the rest pikemen, and with these few, taking our knapsacks and putting in each six pounds of biscuit and a measure of one and a half gallons of wine, with our arms and ammunition; each Captain and soldier—I was among the first setting the example, carrying this food and arms on my back. Not knowing the way, we hoped to get there in two days. it being distant about eight leagues or so, as we were told by two Indians who went with us as guides. Leaving this Fort of St. Augustine in the order above described and with determination on the eighteenth of September, we found the rivers so swollen from the copious rains that it was impossible to ford them and we were obliged to take a circuitous route which had never been used before through swamp and unknown roads to avoid the rivers.

After walking until nine or ten o'clock at night, on the morning of the twentieth, which is the feast of San Mateo, we arrived in sight of the Fort. Having offered prayers to the Blessed Lord and His Holy

Mother, supplicating them to give us victory over these Lutherans, it was agreed that with twenty ladders, which we carried, to assail the Fort. His Divine Majesty had mercy upon us and guided us in such a way that without losing one man and with only one injured (who is now well), we took the Fort with all it contained, killing about two hundred and thirty men, the other ten we took as prisoners to the forest. Among them were many noblemen, one who was Governor and Judge, called Monsieur Laudonnier, a relative of the French Admiral, and who had been his steward. This Laudonnier escaped to the woods and was pursued by one of the soldiers who wounded him, and we know not what has become of him, as he and the others escaped by swimming out to two small boats of the three vessels that were opposite the Fort, with about fifty or sixty persons. I sent them a canonade and call of the trumpet to surrender themselves, vessels and arms. They refused, so with the artillery found in the Fort we sunk one vessel, the others taking up the men went down the river where they had two other vessels anchored laden with provisions, being of the seven sent from France, and which had not yet been unloaded. It did not seem to me right to leave the Fort and pursue them until I had repaired three boats we found in the Fort. The Indians notified them of our actions. As they were so few they took the two best and strongest vessels and sank the other. In three days they had fled, Being informed of this by the Indians, I did not pursue them. Later from the Fort they wrote me that about twenty Frenchmen had appeared in the forest with no clothing but a shirt, and many of them were wounded. It was believed that Monsieur Laudonnier was among them. I have sent word that they make every effort to capture them and bring them to justice. In the Fort were found, among women, creatures and children under fifteen years of age, about fifty persons. It causes me deep sorrow to see them among my people on account of their horrid religious sect, and I fear our Lord would punish me should I use cruelty with them. Eight or ten of the boys were born here.

These French have many friends among the Indians, who show much feeling at their loss, especially for two or three teachers of their hateful doctrine which they taught to the Indian chiefs, who followed them as the Apostles did our Lord. It is a thing of admiration to see how these Lutherans enchanted the poor savage people. I shall use every means to gain the good will of these Indians who were such friends to the French, and there is no reason why I should break with them, and if I can live with them at peace it will be well; they are such traitors, thieves and drunkards, that it is almost impossible to do so. These chiefs and the Indians, their enemies, all show friendship towards me, which I return and shall continue, unless their depredations increase that I may have to do otherwise.

On the 28th of September the Indians notified me that many Frenchmen were about six leagues from here on the coast, that they had lost their vessels and escaped by swimming and in boats. Taking fifty soldiers I was with them next morning at daylight, and, leaving my men in ambush, I took one with me to the banks of the river, because they were on one side and I on the other bank. I spoke to them, told them I was Spanish; they said they were French. They asked me to come over to them either alone or with my partner, the river being narrow. I replied that we did not know how to swim, but that they could safely come to us. They agreed to do so, and sent a man of some intellect, master of a boat, who carefully related to me how they had left their Fort with four galleons and eight small vessels, that each carried twenty-four oars with four hundred picked soldiers and two hundred marines and John Ribaut as General and Monsieur LeGrange, who was General of the Infantry, and other good captains, soldiers and gentlemen, with the intention of finding me on the sea, and if I attempted to land, to land their people on the small boats and capture me. That if they had wanted to land they could easily have done so, but they had not dared and wanted to return to their Fort. That they were overtaken by a hurricane and tempest and were wrecked about twenty or twenty-five leagues from here. That of the four hundred only forty had survived; that the others had perished or were killed by the Indians. That fifty were carried prisoners by the Indians; that John Ribaut with his captain were anchored five leagues from there in the swamp without trees, and he had in the vessel with him two hundred persons, more or less, and they believed them to have perished with all the artillery and ammunition, which was a great deal and good. Part of it was with John Ribaut and what they had, was certainly lost. They were saved, and he asked for himself and companions safe passage to their Fort, since they were not at war with the Spaniards. I then told him how we had taken their Fort and hung all those we found in it, because they had built it without your Majesty's permission and because they were scattering the odious Lutheran doctrine in these Provinces, and that I had war to fire and blood, as Governor and Captain-General of these Provinces, against all those who came to sow this hateful doctrine; representing to him that I came by order of your Majesty to place the Gospel in these parts and to enlighten the natives in all that the Holy Church of Rome says and does so as to save their souls. That I would not give them passage; rather would I follow them by sea and land until I had taken their lives. He begged to be allowed to go with this embassy and that he would return at night swimming, if I would grant him his life. I did so to show him that I was in earnest and because he could enlighten me on many subjects. Immediately after his return to his companions there came a gentleman, a lieutenant of Monsieur Laudonnier, a man well versed and cunning to tempt me. After much talk he offered to give up their arms if I would grant their lives. I told him he could surrender the arms and give themselves up to my mercy, that I might do with them that which our Lord ordered. More than this he could not get from me, and that God did not expect more of me. Thus he returned and they came to deliver up their arms. I had their hands tied behind them and had them stabbed to death, leaving only sixteen, twelve being great big men, mariners whom they had stolen, the other four master carpenters and caulkers—people for whom we have much need, and it seemed to me to punish them in this manner would be serving

God, our Lord, and your Majesty. Hereafter they will leave us free to plant the Gospel, enlighten the natives, and bring them to obedience and submission of your Majesty. The lands being extensive it will be well to make them work fifty years—besides, a good beginning makes a good end, so I have hopes in our Lord that in all He will grant me prosperity and success, so that I and my descendants may give to your Majesty those Kingdoms full and return the people Christians. My particular interest as I have written your Majesty is this: We are gaining great favor with the Indians and will be feared by them, although we make them many gifts.

Considering what John Ribaut had done, I find that within ten leagues of where he was anchored, three of the vessels of his company were lost; whether they were lost or not, they would have landed the people, unloaded what supplies they could, employed themselves in getting out the brass artillery and the upright posts and tackle, if not lost, of the three vessels, rig themselves as best they could, and if the vessel he was on was not lost he will make every effort to come by sea. Should he do so I await him, and with the help of God, he will be lost. He might also go inland with one of the Casiques, his friend, who lives thirty leagues from here, and is very powerful. Should this be the case I will seek him there, because it is not convenient that he and his companions should remain alive. Should he come by sea to the Fort I have the entrance to the Bar mined with two savage canon and guns, so that should they succeed in making an entrance, we can sink them. A brigantine is kept in readiness to capture the people and I shall do all in my power to prevent his escape. The things found in the Fort were only four pieces of brass of about five tons, the canon and guns which had come from France were dismounted and carried to the galleons when they went in search of me. There were found besides twenty-five bronze musket and as much as twenty tons of powder and ammunition for these pieces, about one hundred and sixty barrels of flour, twenty casks of wine. The balance of the supplies had not been unloaded, as they were hesitating whether they should fortify this Port, fearing I should land here, which I could easily have done. Since their arrival they had spent most of their time in debaucheries over the joy felt at the news they had received that northeast of Santa Elena was a range of mountains coming from the Zacatecas where there were great mines of silver. The Indians from those parts had brought them many pieces of silver to the amount of five and six thousand ducats. We found to the amount of three thousand ducats, more or less, in clothes and all kinds of valuables; some hogs, male and female; also sheep and asses; all this was ransacked by the soldiers; nothing escaped them. Besides the two vessels found in the Port we found two near the Bar and two others they had stolen from the Indians, loaded with hides. Of these they had drowned the crews and the cargo had been given to an English vessel to carry it and sell it in England or France, and there remained with them two Englishmen. The French had no mariners by whom to send these vessels. These two Englishmen were hung when the Fort was captured by us. The Englishmen by whom they sent the cargo arrived in port at the Fort we

Old St. Augustine

have taken from them, the early part of August of this year, in a galleon of a thousand tons called the Queen of England, with three heavy tiers of artillery; all who saw her wondered and had never seen a vessel so heavily armed that drew so little water; the other three vessels were smaller. It was agreed between the English and French that as the French awaited help from France that Monsieur Ludovic, who was Governor here, should wait for them until the end of September; failing to return, he, Ludovic, was to go to France in search of them, and that by the month of April they would return with a large fleet, to await and capture the fleet of New Spain, which was forced to pass their Fort; that if aid came, for which they had written to France, they would advise the English who would come to this coast by the month of April. It was for this purpose that I found in the Fort a large vessel and seven small ones, and another five, one or two of which had been stolen, and the four they wished to send to France to have them equipped with men and provisions to join the English and themselves by April; that by that time John Ribaut would have returned and with the eight hundred men who remained he wished to go by January to Los Martyres, about twenty-five leagues from Havana, and there build a fort. They had reconnoitered and found it a very desirable port. This was agreed between them, and that before leaving France John Ribaut was to obtain the order that they should fortify Los Martyres, a strait by which no vessel could enter or depart without being sighted by them. To keep there always in readiness six vessels, it being the best sea in the world for them. That from there they would take Havana, free all the negroes; that they would then send to make the same offer to the Spanish of Porto Rico and all other colonies. All this information I gained from the skilful Frenchman to whom I granted life. They had with them six Portuguese pilots whom they hung when no longer needed; two others had been killed by the Indians, and two were with Ribaut. The river San Mateo, running by the Fort we captured, goes seventy leagues inland and turns to the southeast emptying into the bay of Juan Ponce, and from there to New Spain and the port of San Juan de Luca, where there is only upwards of fifty leagues. In the bay of Juan Ponce they thought next year to build a fort on account of its proximity to New Spain, distant a hundred and fifty leagues and about the same distance from Honduras and as many more from Yucatan, and where with their six vessels they could navigate with ease. On this river are three large Indian towns. The Indians are great friends of the French who have been there three times in search of corn. These French landed there in great need of supplies, having only enough to carry them eight days. Corn they found scarce and took it almost by force. The Indians themselves are great thieves—a poor but brave people. All the Indians are not more friendly to them than to us, and I will not consent to take a grain of corn from them, but prefer to give them of what I may have. I consider this country so vast and fertile and the danger from enemies and corsaires so great and that they can appropriate to themselves the land lying north of here near New Foundland, of which they are already lords, and can be sustained by them with ease. Everything should be done to aid me instead of cutting me off, and your Majesty must be undeceived and know that I am much better able than your Majesty to enlarge and aggrandize these your Kingdoms. This Port is 29½ degrees, and the San Mateo which we captured is 31 degrees. The French and their pilots were mistaken. I have had it taken by the sun on land. From here to the Cape of Canaveral there are fifty leagues, three rivers, two ports between here and Havana, one hundred miles, more or less, which are navigable in boats among the keys of Canavarel and Los Martyres, and from there to Havana. I agree to take the good field pieces which we have captured from the French, and one hundred men go along the borders of the coast, the boats by sea, anchoring at night near land among the keys of Canaveral where the sea is as smooth as a river, with the boats they will be able to discover among the keys the best port and surroundings to build a fort. So that with the one in Havana and this one we can at all times guard against the enemy and their entering to fortify themselves. Nor should we expect fleets or boats of the Indians. With the people of Havana, Santo Domingo and Pedro de la Roda, whom I shall have to come to my assistance, I will have until the last of March to build it, then with these vessels go over to Havana and seek these people. Having discovered the Port, and on the arrival of Pedro de la Roda in Havana he will find his vessels which I do not propose to take out of that Port, also his men, so that he may return to Spain as strong as when he left there. That I shall place one hundred and fifty Spaniards in possession to guard against the Indians who are great warriors and whose good will we must gain. Then, by the 1st of April, I shall return to these two Forts, and in six or eight days I shall again take to the sea. By the month of March, leaving these two Forts well equipped and guarded each with three hundred men, I shall go in vessels that draw little water which I will soon have here, most of them the ones taken from the French. I will man as many as I can with five hundred soldiers and one hundred mariners, found a town at Santa Elena, which is fifty leagues from here, and has within three leagues of it three Ports and rivers, the largest of six fathoms of water, the other four fathoms; admirable Ports and the one we call Santa Elena is the third, the one the French occupied is very small; the three are navigable, one within the other, so that he who is lord of one is lord of the three. It is the best place to build a fort leaving three hundred men to finish it, pass on up the bay to Santa Maria, which is 36 degrees, one hundred and thirty leagues beyond Santa Elena; then on to the land of the Indians which is in Mexico, fortify another fort and leave another two hundred soldiers. This will be the key to all the fortifications of this country, because from those to the new land it does not have to be founded. Inland, about eighty leagues, are to be found a range of mountains, at their base an arm of sea which leads to the New Land. This arm of the sea enters the New Land which is navigable seventy leagues where there is another sea turning northeast and we suspect it leads to the South Sea. The Indians send many cattle from New Spain which were found on these plains by Francisco Basques Coronado. They carried the hides to the New Land in canoes to sell to the French in exchange for barter. From here, in the past two years, they have carried in their fishing boats more than six thousand hides. The French can go from here in their vessels to the foot of the mountain range four hundred leagues from the mines of San Martin and New Galicia and can mine them to their heart's content. It would be well to fix our frontier lines here, gain the water-way of the Bahamas and work the mines of New Spain. This key and strength is necessary that your Majesty should become Lord of all of it, because by it you will be master of the world. I have written to Pedro del Castillo to send me three hundred soldiers and supplies for eight hundred persons. It would be useless not to have the three hundred soldiers to serve your Majesty and to provide the necessaries. Thus on, from the first of February, your Majesty can send a hundred mariners and the equipments and let them bring everything necessary to found a town in the Bay of Juan Ponce, as this river is part of San Mateo, which we captured from the enemy. Eighteen leagues inland from this bay, and from one bay to the other, we can easily trade with the multitude of Indians that are there and make them soon learn the Gospel of our Lord Jesus Christ. In this Bay of Juan Ponce is the Province of Appalache, an indomitable people with whom the Spaniards have never been able to treat. Thus will all difficulties be overcome so far as New Galicia which is about three hundred leagues, and so many more to Vera Cruz, and the same distance to Yucatan. From there this town will be provided with corn, as there is much of it. As we found the place and build a good City, there will be no need of founding others in Florida. We will then proceed to the New Land, easily work the many mines of silver which are found there, and are the mines of the Zacatecas. In a few years the silver worked from them will support this country and be a treasure to your Majesty and a suburb of Spain which can be reached in forty days from these Kingdoms. With the scarcity of supplies in the Forts we are suffering much hunger as the grain was burned and so, unless we receive aid soon, we shall suffer terribly. I trust your Majesty is satisfied that we serve you faithfully and with love and in all truth. Without extending myself further, but promising to keep you advised of all that may happen, may God protect your Majesty, increasing your royal Catholic personage with greater kingdoms and possessions as Christianity has need of and your servants desire it should be.

From these Provinces of Florida from the banks of San Pelayo and Fort of St. Augustine, October 15th, 1565. PEDRO MENENDEZ DE AVILES.

CHAPTER III.

A. D. 1583-1596-1598.

Report of Fernando Mirando, agent to the King—Complains of Governor—Espionage over vessels—Gives account of the work of the negroes—Haste makes it necessary to employ soldiers in repairing the Fort for which they were paid—Partial failure of crops increases the cost of living—Report of Bartolome De Arguellas giving account of rebellious Indians—Some of those captured were sent to Havana to be executed, others to be imprisoned—Casiques render obedience to the Governor who assures them of his good intentions—Report of Pedro Pertrene to the King—Is newly called to take charge of a company of Infantry in the Garrison of Florida—Salary not sufficient to meet expenses of living, recalls his long service to the King, and asks for increase of pay—Letter from Dona Maria Menendez, Casique, to the King—Asks for assistance in meeting the necessary expenses for instruction of the Indians in Christianity and good government.

A. D. 1583.

Fernando Miranda and Rodrego Junco, assistant Agent, who was of these Kingdoms, to His Majesty:

After the Governor had given a decree of the same suspension, we asked him that until your Majesty should otherwise provide, we be allowed to continue in office and watch over your Majesty's interest. Another thing which occurs to us to inform your

Majesty: Yesterday there sailed from this Port for Havana a vessel belonging to some one in Havana, and the Governor made every effort to see if we had sent any papers by her—he searched the vessel and not wishing to give testimony, we understood he did not wish any letters sent, and so we dared not write more. We felt that this would be sufficient for your Majesty to place the remedy and investigate the cause, and punish the culprit.

In the two years that your Majesty's negroes have been here, they have made a platform for the artillery of this Fort of an indestructible wood—as the one they had previous to this rotted away in two years. They have made a blacksmith shop, and whatever repairs were needed on the Fort. Ten of the best of them were sent to Santa Elena to saw boards to cover that Fort which needed it. On beginning the work it was found that the whole Fort was in such a damaged condition it was necessary to tear it all down and rebuild as quickly as possible. On account of the haste required the soldiers were obliged to help for which work they were paid. It was completed in four months, during which time the negroes had to be fed on bread, meat and wine. Besides they have helped to build a church here, sawed lumber for the building of many dwellings, and have cleared the woods to some extent for planting. The first crop not being good, caused extra expense of food and ammunition which was given them—but for the past six months they have been fed on the harvest made, with no other expense but the oil and salt. They have corn enough to last until the next harvest, and all the expense incurred to the end of June of the present year is six thousand five hundred reals, from the Treasury of your Majesty —because, although there have been some other expenses, we have availed ourselves of advantages we had after having had recourse to what has been offered to your Majesty's service. About six months ago eleven of these negroes were hired to soldiers of this Fort, without the knowledge of the Treasurer, rendering an account of this to the Governor. It is about a year and a half since we notified the Governor that he should not keep these accounts, but as provided by your Majesty they should be sent to this Court. He has never sent them. Your Majesty will act as best suits him in this affair of our suspension; we again implore your Majesty to give us a hearing, and some satisfaction, since we are left in this sterile country without the means of sustenance. May God preserve your Majesty for many years with great aggrandizement. FERNANDO MIRANDA.

St. Augustine, August 20th. 1583.

Your Majesty:

As the Governor, Don Domingo Martinez Avendano, has been sending your Majesty an account of the proceedings of our journey, I have not done so until now, that we have landed in these Provinces of Florida, and seen the condition of things, the people of the Garrison and the natives. It was a blessing of God that it was all quiet and peaceful, and the Governor with much gentleness and discretion entered, and proceeded well, to support the service of your Majesty. It was a very fortunate thing, as many of the culprits had made threats, which if carried into effect, would have resulted disastrously—but they had not the heart to carry them out, although a number of the worst criminals were out of the country. Of those who remained, ten were captured, and with their accusations were sent by Captain Francisco Salazar to Havana, in the custody of a trusted lieutenant and twelve soldiers, as guards, so that they may be executed there and accomplish your Majesty's will. With this imprisonment and a public reprimand made by the Governor to the other Indians, all of which remain quiet. Being overcome with fear, I understand they will return promptly to their employment, and your Majesty will be well served. The Casiques of this country came to render obedience to the Governor, who caressed them and instructed them of the manner and order in which they were to attend to your Majesty's work—he told them he wished to visit them in their homes, and the good intentions and desires he brings of attending to your service and the proofs he has already given of them. We entertain great hopes that all will soon be settled. From Havana they dispatched to the Treasurer Juan Menendez Marquez to be present at the paying off of the employees of this Garrison. While the Governor intended to have me assume control of this collection, he seemed to change his mind, and I came here with him, where I remain attending to the duties under my charge until he thinks that I may go out and make use of the license your Majesty granted me if nothing more occurs. May Our Lord guard the person of your Royal Catholic Majesty, as we have need of you.

BARTOLOME DE ARGUELLAS.

St. Augustine, Florida, July 6th, 1596.

Your Majesty: A. D. 1598.

I do not wish to make a long report in this letter, as I understand a detailed account of all that occurs in these provinces will be made by your Majesty's Governor, Gonzalo Menendez Canso, who in every thing appertaining to your Majesty's service and welfare is proceeding with caution—reforming, arranging everything in the most approved manner, discovering as he goes, all the secrets of the service, and governing himself in accordance. He has strong and brave resolutions, as I know, having communicated them to me, and given me an account of his good intentions.

Having served your Royal Highness for twenty-six years in this part of your Royal Fleet, in charge of your Captains-General the Adelantado Pedro Menendez Aviles, Diego Flores Valdez, Cristobal Eraso, and Alvarez Flores de Quinones, as Officer in the companies in which I served as Lieutenant of the Governor of the Castle, under Diego Fernandez de Guinones, in Havana. Being in that City, retired in my home, I was called by the above mentioned Governor to give and honor me with one of your Majesty's companies of infantry who served in this Garrison of Florida. In his absence to Guale to the chastising of the Indians, who so horribly killed six priests of the San Franciscan Order, he left me in his place. Of the spoils which are usually divided, he has shared with me moderately, but even with these, and the two hundred ducats I have as salary, and the advantages given me, I cannot sustain myself, nor assist at the obligations of such Captains, on account of every thing in the land being so dear—provisions are the same—and the servant we had, was taken from us by your Governor. I implore your Majesty to attend to the above mentioned facts, and as my desire is to end my life in your Royal Service—and that I may live and keep up my obligations I may be given some help toward my expenses, and that I may be allowed a servant, as is customary with all Captains serving in this Garrison, and trusting that your Majesty will grant me these things as are granted to all who serve you with good will. God preserve your Royal Person as I desire and Christianity needs you.

PEDRO PERTRENE.

St. Augustine, Florida, February 20th, 1598.

Your Majesty:

My poverty and the frequency with which the Indians, both Christians and infidels, gather at my home to be instructed in matters concerning their conversion, and other important things concerning the good Government need with the Governor of these Provinces, places me under the necessity of asking your Majesty to assist me in the expenses I am obliged to incur with the Indians, as is certified to by the report accompanying this letter which implores your Majesty to assist and see to this need, since from it will result the coming of the Indians with more heartiness to become Christians and in this way guard the faith. Your Royal Highness being merciful. That I may do in all the above mentioned what is just and right, I also implore your Majesty to send me a letter of friendship that the Indians may see the good feeling which exists between your Majesty and ourselves. God grant you may have all graces.

Florida, February 20th, 1598.

CHAPTER IV.

A. D. 1598.

Extract from an official report made by Gonzalo Menendez Canso, Governor and Captain General of the Provinces of Florida, concerning the murder of six priests of the San Franciscan Order by the Indians—Lieutenant Eciga sent to see if any of the priests are still living—Ascertains that there is one, but is refused permission to see him—After much persuasion and many threats Friar Fray Francisco is delivered—Makes statement as to death of the others, but is forbidden by the canons of the Church to reveal all — Juan Ximanes, a Notary Public and secretary, swears to the investigation of several Indians through an interpreter — Indian Lucas is found to have been present and participated in the killing of Fray Blas for which he is condemned to be executed.

DONA MARIA MENENDEZ—CASIQUE.

This is a good and faithful copy taken from one of the official reports made by Gonzalo Menendez Canes, Governor and Captain-General of these Provinces of Florida to His Majesty, concerning the death of the Religious of the Order of San Francisco, who perished at the hands of the Indians who revolted. Its tenor is:

In the city of St. Augustine, Province of Florida, July 1st, 1598, Gonzalo Menendez Canes, Governor and Captain-General for the King our Lord, says: That in the month of October past of 1597, he was notified of an uprising of the Indians of the Peninsula of Guale. They had refused to obey your Majesty, and killed the Religious of the Order of San Francisco sent out to convert and teach them, and that he had made every and the greatest efforts, having gone in person with a number of infantry, ammunition and water craft to said peninsula, to investigate and punish the cases, and ascertain the cause the Indians had for committing such an atrocious crime. Although he made all the ravages he could, acting upon advices received, he could not punish them more for the time being, nor could he capture a live Indian, except one, an interpreter, from whom they could get no information further than that the Religious had been killed, as will be seen by his declaration. Seeing the importance of ascertaining the root and cause of the killing of these Religious, and if any were still living—and why they had lost obedience to your Majesty, he has made the boldest efforts possible, going by way of the Luna. Finding the Casiques in conference, we agreed to send them presents and keepsakes, to induce them to let us know and understand if any of the Religious or Friars were still living that we might ransom them, sending to offer them even interest for them, and also sending a launch with some of the infantry to the Fort Santa Elena, distant fifty leagues from this Garrison, to enlist the Casique of that country, on account of the friendship he has shown the Spaniards, and because he has Indian warriors, and being so near he could do much damage to the Peninsula of Guale. Lieutenant Exiga, who went in the launch, found him and treated with him to make war and do all the damage possible to said peninsula and ascertain if any of them were living—bestowing upon him many gifts from your Majesty's treasury that he might go. It was agreed that Lieutenant Exiga should return to the Casique in sixty days, and ascertain what military exploits he had had, and what success. Being a matter of so much importance to your Majesty, Lieutenant Exiga left this port on the 23rd of May, with two launches, with infantry and ammunition to accomplish the agreement made with the Casique. On the 24th, one day after leaving this fort, having gone as far as the Bar of Asae, twenty leagues from here, he was caught in a storm and hurricane, forcing him to put into harbor in distress. The storm did so much damage to the food and ammunition they carried, that he was obliged to strike with the launch for the shore of San Mateo. Nothwithstanding all the above mentioned, he continued his voyage to the port Santa Elena, there taking another launch in better condition for making the journey, leaving his in bad condition grounded on the beach. Having arrived at Santa Elena and seen and spoken to the Casique who delivered to him four gentlemen, he said he had taken from four Indians of the Peninsula of Gaule where he went to make war. That three other Indians had captured the Casique of Carague, who had accompanied him, with the intent of making war. In the same way he certifies that they had alive in the Peninsula of Gaule, near Solofina, one of the six friars, named Toray Francisco de Avila. Having learned this he came coasting along the shore and ports of Guale, to see if any Indians should come out to speak to them. None appeared, until he came to Tolomato where he saw one, who by much coaxing and presenting of gifts and reasoning, succeeded in getting him to tell what he knew. Finally they learned from him that the said Friar was still living. They paid the Indian to take a letter to him, and they would await the reply—he did so, and in the meantime they amused themselves coasting along the shores of Tolomato, until the Indian returned with some of the Casiques, whom they begged would show them the Friar, that they might certify to his being alive, and treat with them for his ransom. At first, although they had heaped the Indians with gifts, they would neither accept of the gifts nor promise to deliver the Friar, unless in return for certain boys, sons of some of the Casiques, who had been brought to Governor Domingo Martinez Avendano, as hostages. As better security Lieutenant Exiga promised to bring their boys within thirty days as ransom for the Friar, also a quantity of hatchets and spades they asked for. Lieutenant Exiga returned to Port Tolomato in fifteen days, and began treaty with Casiques for the ransom of the Friar, and although he heaped gifts upon them with a free hand, it made no impression. They are such liars and traitors, and all their treaties are founded on treachery and cunning. Seeing that they did not intend to keep their word and deliver the priest, he found it necessary to change his tactics and show anger, swearing that unless they did deliver the prisoner they would send for three hundred soldiers and would run them through with the sword, cut down all their crops and follow them to Tama. After these threats they promised to deliver the Priest at once, which they did. After receiving him, and having him in their power, Lieutenant Exiga made reprisal of the hostages he carried, and of seven other Indians he had detained on the launch until he saw what sucess he was going to have. Four of these Indians are sons and brothers of Casiques. The Governor holds them and has brought them to this city where they are at present, and where he protests he will investigate and take their declarations as to the manner of death the other friars suffered—where, in what form, and for what cause? Finding any of them to have taken part in this crime, to punish them and do justice to the service of your Majesty, and that this punishment may serve as an example to them, as they have at other times committed these treacheries, killing captains and officers and other persons. This I provide and sign from his hand, Gonzalo Menendez Vanso, by order of His Lordship the Governor and Captain-General.   JUAN XIMENES.

Later the said Governor and Captain-General ordered me, the secretary, that I should go to the Monastary of San Francisco, of this city, and in his name ask the custodian priest of said house, Fray Francisco Marron, to give permission to Fray Francisco de Avila, who had been sent to teach and convert the Indians, that under the oath which is administered to the Religious of his Order, he declared how his companions were killed, what he has seen and heard, and the causes that have moved them to commit such a crime as the killing of the priests. To deny obedience, and tell only what he knows and understands of the matter. They continued the examination, so that all the above may be certified as the truth. This I provide and sign in his name—and from the declaration of the father custodian might result many worthy considerations in questioning the Indians.
                    GONZALO MENENDEZ CANSO.

Later—The present notary public went to the Monastery of San Francisco, of this city, read and showed the decree above disposed of by his Lordship the Governor and Captain-General Gonzalo Menendez Canso, to Fray Francisco Marron, custodian of the provinces, who said: that mindful that Fray Francisco de Avila was one of the friars sent out to teach and convert in the Peninsula of Guale, and as the Lord, Our God, had seen proper to deliver him from being killed by the Indians, as his companions had been, and as a person who knew the habits and manners of the Indians, and knew their language, he deemed it wise to give him freedom to say and declare all he considered would be to the service of God of the killing of his companions—except in cases and things criminal where his rights of priesthood prohibited, such as death by the cutting of members—and this I say and sign in his name—Fray Francisco Marron— in my presence.

St. Augustine, Fla., July 20th. 1598.

JUAN XIMENES.

Gonzalo Menendez Canso, Governor and Captain-General for his Majesty in these Provinces, ordered to be called Fray Francisco de Avila that in virtue of the permission granted him by the Custodian Fray Francisco Marron, to say and declare all he knows concerning the killing of his companions by the Indians, and of his imprisonment and captivity—whether his person was badly treated, and all that had occurred worthy of relating—so as to punish such crime as it deserves to be.

Fray Francisco de Avila said: Although it was true Fray Marron had granted him permission to speak, he could not make use of it, in cases so grave and criminal as the present—it was prohibited him by the sacred canons of priesthood, to attest in such crimes, because it would force him to say that which might condemn some, and so, he did not wish to speak or declare in this case, not to fall into any error. Besides being mindful that the Governor had brought seven Indians from the peninsula at the time of his ransom, to this city, he could know and understand from them all that they might claim. This he said, and I sign it in his name. FRAY FRANCISCO DE AVILA.

In my presence— JUAN XIMENES,
Notary Public.

Later—The Governor and Captain-General Gonzalo Menendez Canso, in order to investigate, had appeared before him Gaspar de Salas, an interpreter of the Indians of Guale who, having been sworn in the proper form, gave promise to tell the truth and nothing but the truth—and that he would declare all that he was ordered to say to the Indians who claim to give information; that he will say and declare all that said Indians say in reply, under the oath that he has taken.

Later the Governor ordered to appear before him one of the seven Indians who were brought from the peninsula, to whom the following questions were put: From where do you come and what is your name? He came from Tupique and that his name was Lucas. Are you a Christian? Yes. The name of your parents, are they, or have they been Casiques? His father's name was Felipe, and he was Casique of Tupique. Where was he from? He was a native of the town of Tupique. Had there been any priest there? There had been one named Fray Blas Rodriguez. Tell and declare what had become of Fray Blas? That about ten or eleven moons past, eight Casiques held a conference, they were Asao, Tolafo, Atmehe, Fulo, Tupique and Alnate. When night came they killed the Priest. A helping hand was given them by a chief called Pisiache, that he might kill him with a hatchet, with which he gave him a blow on the head, from which wound he died almost immediately. Afterward they buried him in the church. Say and declare what cause they had for killing this priest? That Micas and Casiques said they killed him because he was artful and took away their enchantment or witchcraft, and would not allow them to have more than one wife.

Did you hear them say anything else? No. Did he know Fray Miguel de Annon, and Fray Antonio Lego, among the teachers of Guale, and Fray Pedro de Corpa, among the teachers of Tolomato, and Fray Francisco de Avila, among the teachers of Ospo?

I have known them all, and they have been killed. Fray Miguel had his hands tied behind him, but he did not know if they had killed him—Fray Antonio was tied, but he does not know how he was killed—he had heard it said that they killed him with wooden weapons, and that Fray Pedro Corpa two Casiques had killed in the night while sleeping; that Fray Francisco de Avila they had not killed, but had him captive near Tolofino until he should be ransomed by the Governor.

Was Fray Francisco well or ill-treated in the prison?

Some times they beat him with sticks and abused him. They sometimes fed him, but not always, and when they did it was on the leaves and tendrils of vines.

Had he seen or heard it said why they killed these Priests and ill-treated Fray Francisco de Avila?

He knew no more than what he had already stated, that the Micos and Casiques said they were artful and did not wish them to have more than one wife, and that they reproved them.

Do you know where the ornaments belonging to the Church are, such as the chalices and other things used by the priests?

They were all divided up in such a way, that nothing is left of them.

Was he present at the death of Fray Blas and the other priests when they were killed?

He arrived in time to see Fray Blas die—the others he had not seen, but had heard it said that they had been killed as he stated above.

Had he seen or heard any of his companions who were brought with him, say they were present at the killing of the priests?

One from Tolomato, named Francisco, he heard him say he had seen Fray Pedro Corpa after he was killed —the rest he does not know.

All this the said Gaspar Salas said and declared as interpreted under the oath which he has taken. He does not sign because he does not know how to write.

GONZALO MENENDEZ CANSO.

In the presence of JUAN XIMENES,
Notary Public.

For further investigation of the above, the Governor and Captain-General had appeared before him the other Indian, said to be named Francisco and native of Tolomato, and by the said interpreter under oath had him declare the following:

Are you a Christian, and who are your parents?

I am a Christian, my name is Francisco, my mother is nearly related to the Casique and my father is dead.

What priest was teacher at Tolomato?

Fray Pedro Corpa, and I knew him there for some time.

What became of Fray Pedro Corpa?

He was killed while sleeping, with wooden weapons, and he was killed by one of the chief Casiques of the Salcachecos.

Did you see him killed, or were you present at his death?

I was far away, but I heard it said that this Micos of Tolomato and Don Juan, his heir, had sent to have him killed. I went there, but he was already dead.

Did the little dress which you wear belong to some religious of that peninsula?

Yes, but I do not know to which one, I ransomed it from one of the Casiques.

What was the cause of the killing of the priests?

The cause was, that they reproved Don Juan, heir of Tolomato. By his cunning he had the other Casiques meet with him, and there was an uprising in the land, and these killings were done.

Did you know Fray Miguel Annon, and Fray Antonio Lego in the conversion and teachings of Guale, and Father Berahula, and Fray Francisco de Avila?

I knew them all—they had been killed by the Indians, except Fray Francisco de Avila, who was ransomed by the Governor.

Tell and declare what manner of death they have given these religious?

Fray Miguel and Fray Antonio Lego were killed with wooden weapons—he had so heard it said—the others he did not know.

While in prison was Fray Francisco de Avila well treated?

I have heard it said that he was badly treated by the Indians of Tolofino—they whipped him—the boys teased him. He ate badly, because the Indians had little food, and some times he was forced to eat vines and tendrils.

Do you know where the ornaments of the Church are, and the other belongings of the priests?

All the ornaments and clothes of the priests were divided among them all, and the Indians had carried them to their country inland.

Do you know if any of the Indians with you here, were present at the killing of the priests?

I have heard it said that the Indian Lucas, son of Don Felipe, was present when they killed Fray Blas—that about the others he does not know. All of which the said Gaspar Salas Atiqui says and declares according to his oath given, and because the Indian Francisco said so, and did not sign because he did not know how. GONZALO MENENDEZ CANSO.

In the presence of JUAN XIMENES,
Notary Public.

Later the Governor had appear before him the Indian Bartolome, of the Peninsula of Guale, who with other Indians was sent to the peninsula with a message from him to the Micos and Casiques, to the better ascertain, if any of the priests were still living. Although he had been sent, he did not return with the message, until after the treaty for the ransom of Fray Francisco de Avila. He stated that they would not let him come—that he wanted to come and stay with the Governor; that he did not wish to remain among the Indians, and through the interpreter, Atiqui, he declared the following:

Where are you from, and what is your name, and are you a Christian?

My name is Bartolome; I am a Christian and a native of Tolomato. I was sent about eight months ago, by this Governor, with a message to the Micos and Casiques of the peninsula; they would not let me come back, making threats that they would kill me.

During the time you were in the peninsula tell what you know and heard said of the killing of the priests; what kind of death they were given?

I heard that Fray Pedro Corpa was killed at night in his cell, with wooden weapons, and that Fray Miguel, Fray Antonio and Fray Blas were also killed with wooden weapons. That Fray Francisco de Avila, who had just been brought as ransom, was the first one taken prisoner. They stuck him with their arrows, but God did not let him die of the wounds. They would have killed him as they did the others but for the intervention of the Casique of Tulapo, who took him from the Indians, saying at the time that he was his father, and as such he would protect him.

What was the motive and cause of the killing?

I heard it was because they reproved them; that the priests were crafty, and did not care for them, and did not wish them to have more than one wife.

Where are the ornaments and appurtenances of the Church?

They were divided among them, those from the interior carrying many, and many were also broken, and the children tore and destroyed them.

Did you hear it said whether Lucas, the son of the Casique Don Felipe, or any of the other Indians brought in with you were present at the killing of the priests?

I heard that Lucas was there at the killing. I know nothing more.

How was Fray Francisco de Avila treated while a prisoner?

I have heard it said that in Tufina and Chacalaga the boys would chase him through the streets perfectly naked and whip him with horsewhips, and that he was starving to death, because the Indians had little to eat themselves and gave him none. All this Gaspar Salas says and declares to have been said by the Indian Bartolome under the oath which he has taken, and it is the truth; he cannot sign, not knowing how to do so.   GONZALO MENENDEZ CANSO.

In the presence of   JUAN XIMENES,
                          Notary Public.

For further investigation of the above, the Governor and Captain-General had appear before him another of the seven Indians who through the same interpreter said and declared the following: (This declaration is not given.)

In view of said declarations of these proceedings, the crime falls upon Lucas the Indian, son of the Casique de Tuqui, for having been present and participated in the killing of Fray Blas, who was sent to convert the people of Tupiqui. I must condemn him by this my decree, sentenced according to his declaration, with the penalty of death. The justice which I order shall be done him is: That when he leaves the jail where he now is, it shall be with a rope around his neck, his hands tied behind him, and with a loud voice it must be proclaimed to the public his crime; that he be taken to the gallows, already prepared for this purpose, and that there he shall be hung by the neck and strangled until dead. Because, thus is it well to punish with real justice those who dare to commit such crimes, and as an example to the other Indian natives of these provinces that they may not commit similar crimes. So do I pronounce sentence and command. And if the said Lucas is not mindful of receiving baptism and should not die repenting, and in the Catholic faith, I order that he be hung and after his death his body be burned to powder.

Regarding the other six Indians detained for this cause, proceedings will not continue for the present against them—they being boys under age. We shall so send and notify the Indian Lucas.

GONZALO MENENDEZ CANSO.

Alonzo Diaz de Badajoz, Sergeant-Major of this Fort and Garrison of St. Augustine:

I order you by this sentence, which will be shown you by Juan Ximenes, Notary Public, against the Indian Lucas. prisoner in this city, that he shall be executed as is stated in this sentence, because it so pleaseth his Majesty. This execution is done in justice to his Majesty, and must be so accomplished.

GONZALO MENENDEZ CANSO.

St. Augustine, July 29th, 1598.

Notary Public.

Before me JUAN XIMENES,

CHAPTER V.

A. D. 1600.

Letter from Father Francisco Parga to the King, as one of eleven monks sent out by his Majesty to spread the Gospel—Eighty churches in different Missions—Complaint of lazy Indians—Avarice of the Governor causes dissatisfaction and suffering among the garrison and impedes the work—Unnecessary war with Indians — People desire the Governor's removal — Fray Baltazar Lopez has labored for twelve years converting many Indians, among them the Casique, Don Jaun, who stands highly among his people and has quelled many uprisings—Letter from Juan Nunez Rios—Complains of Governor—Who allows one Juan Garcia to represent him—People forced to buy of this Garcia who takes all advantages—Begs for an open port that the people may be allowed to go back and forth and trade—Antonio Menendez Canso writes to his Majesty complaining of injustice by the Governor, and asks to be allowed to serve his Majesty elsewhere—Letter to his Majesty from Fray Blas De Montes imploring that he may be allowed to come to Spain for retirement—Gives account of a fire which burned the church among other houses— Reports slow progress with the Indians and advises that a Bishop be sent to administer sacrament of confirmation — Report of Gonzalo Menendez Canso to his Majesty—A shipmaster bearing dis-

patches from New Spain shipwrecked in a dreadful storm—He and his crew escape in a boat—Governor aids them from the Royal treasury—Arrival of the Auditor for his Majesty—Garrison abounding in fruits and grain—Death of a Christian Indian, Don Jaun—Fray Lopez returns from New Spain in good health—Money brought to establish a hospital—More money needed for Garrison expenses—Report of Francisco Redondo Villegas, Officer of Customs and Auditor for his Majesty—Complains of not being treated with the respect due to Royal officers—Finds affairs in a muddled condition — Soldiers well drilled — Much land under cultivation which will be needed as wages are small and rations insufficient.

PATRON LETTER FROM FRAY FRANCISCO PARGA, OF THE SAN FRANCISCAN ORDER, TO THE KING.

Your Majesty:

This is a duplicate of a letter sent your Majesty by a vessel which left this port of St. Augustine in the month of February of this year via Havana. I wrote giving an account as I was one of the eleven monks sent by your Majesty to spread the Gospel and teach the natives of this country. When we arrived we were assigned to different places or posts, each one trying his utmost and best to do what he could for the redemption of these souls. It being such an arduous and difficult life, having to traverse on foot, bad roads, with little or nothing to eat at times, that little fruit has yet been yielded, although the harvest, which we hope eventually to reap for the Lord, is worth the trials and sacrifices made, as we know that

Old St. Augustine

He suffered death and passion to redeem the souls and rejoiceth over the salvation of one; how much more should we be willing to suffer for the conversion of so many souls as there are in this country and whom we hope to save with the help of God? And so I say that while your Majesty has control of these lands as the Religious have charge of this Garrison in time of need, and they also help to support the Church under their care and the ornaments and other things necessary for the worship of the Divine Lord, not having for this purpose any income from your Royal Finance. There are more than eighty churches which have been built in the different missions and others under construction. We are moved to do this to encourage the Indians who are incapable of good conceptions and obedience. They have always had their ministry so that they listen with little appreciation to what we preach and teach, in grave detriment to the poor newly converted Indians, notwithstanding that our teaching and converting accrues to their own good, as we aid and provide for them in their time of hunger, and when crops have failed. The Indians are so lazy and improvident that if we did not take care of the crops after planting they would have nothing. They do not even save the seed for another planting. Of the Governor I wish to say as little as possible, but the misery, impediment and calamities among Indians and Christians is due to his avarice, and if the poor Spaniards who are in the Garrison of St. Augustine had not the hope that your Majesty would be informed in some way and send them relief from the fearful calamity which this Garrison is suffering, the affliction among the married men as well as the single would become unendurable. They dare not, under any circumstances, send you information, as it would cost them their lives, and so they have prayed and implored me as Chaplain, who live from day to day upon the charity of your Royal Treasury, and have to render a strict account or others would slander us, and our account of the war and other matters must be true. The war with the Indians where many have been killed and many brought in as prisoners was uncalled for and the Indians at "Cabeza de Martyres" are much incensed. As it is a place where many vessels are wrecked, the Spaniards have taken whole crews and kept them until ransomed. We fear the Indians of that place will do much damage to vessels passing to and fro. We feel very sorry that the present Governor has shown so much anger and resentment towards the Indians and has sent your Majesty such meagre accounts of the true condition of this Garrison. It is swampy, little inhabited by Indians, and the roads difficult to traverse. The Bar is a rough one; there are said to be better ones on this coast towards the north. I have not seen them, but have heard through Fray Baltazar Lopez, Vicar of that Island, who has been there for twelve years working in the conversion of souls, with other Friars who came with him, and who have left for New Spain. He alone remains at his post, much encouraged, as he has mastered the Indian language; it is of great help to him in preaching. He has converted many who frequent the sacraments of confession and communion. Had it not been for him and through his persuasions, having converted and taught the Casique Don Juan, there would have been a terrible uprising among the Indians, and probably not a Spaniard left. Thus, by the industry and influence of Fray Baltazar over Don Juan, who is highly in favor of christianity and all civilized ideas, this trouble was averted. Don Juan has sent relief to the people of this garrison in times of famine. I recognize in Fray Baltazar that spiritual zeal for the service of God and your Majesty that this land may be converted, increase in civilization and aggrandize your kingdom. As Fray Baltazar's experience is of long standing, it has been decided that he write to your Majesty and give a full account of all the happenings. To this letter of his, which I shall remit to your Majesty, you can give full credit, as he speaks scientifically and from long experience.

Your Majesty:

As a final remedy and forced by necessity and worry which we poor citizens of this garrison suffer ever since the arrival of Gonzalo Menendez Canso, we come to implore you, as King and Christian, not to permit that your subjects and vassals be so ill treated and afflicted by those who govern here, since your Majesty in your Cedulas always orders the contrary. There being no corporation as in other cities of like size to whom we can appeal for protection, I take the liberty of writing this. We have not done so before, and gone on suffering all that is possible for us to suffer, because we understood you had been informed by other parties, and we hoped and waited daily to be delivered by your sending some one else who would proceed in a different manner, and thus we poor citizens would receive better treatment at his hands, and enable us to proceed in better condition to advance your interests which have been decreasing and losing ever since the said Governor came. Much of the land that was gained from the Indians, and who themselves had become quiet and peaceful, has been lost. I came to this country in the year 1568, twenty years ago, with others from your Kingdom, to aid and succor, as was commanded by your Majesty in transferring us to these Provinces, having assisted and served in them on all occasions which have presented themselves at Port Elena and St. Augustine. I married a daughter of one of the settlers who was here and had come enthused by the promises made by the previous Governors, but who spent his life eking out a meagre existence for his wife and children by taking advantage of the license which at that time was granted the citizens of going abroad to seek work which was so much needed. This Governor has withdrawn this license and forces us to remain in the town proper. The town is frequently left to the government of his cousin who calls himself Juan Garcia and whom he brought with him to this Province with a large stock of merchandise which he sells at exorbitant prices and he, the Governor, collects all payments. Before this Governor came we were paid off, but since his assumption of affairs he forces us to buy all we need of this cousin, and the Governor informs us that if we do not obey his order in this we must go without. On pay day he keeps all our pay saying we have already spent it. If one of the soldiers is sick requiring anything and sends to ask for money

Old St. Augustine 55

to get the needed medicine the Governor refuses to give it, forcing him to buy it of Juan Garcia. All law suits or troubles of any kind which arise are brought before the Governor by this same Juan Garcia, who seems to be supreme. It is understood that the vast estate is a joint one of Juan Garcia and Governor Menendez Canso. My house was burned, as can be testified by any of the inhabitants, fearing to notify Juan Garcia of the fact. I sent to him and asked him with all due respect to come, accompanied by the Mayor, who is the only representative of the law, and see the condition I was in. For this act he has levied upon me for fifty maravedies and six months" imprisonment in the Fort. That I must appear before him, and he has worried me in many other ways. He has taken from us the only means of making a living for our wives and children and refuses to grant us any rights whatsoever, except those which in your Cedula are so plain he is obliged to grant them. And yet he grants all rights to Mexico. It is a great injustice not to allow us the same privileges. We trust that being so far from us and it takes so long to inform you, that you will have mercy upon us and immediately send some one to replace this Governor. One who will treat us with more kindness and justice. We implore you to grant the privileges of an open port, that we may be allowed to go back and forth and trade, so as to enable us to make a living. Others would write to you imploring the same grace, only all fear to do so, as we run great risk of having the Governor intercept our letters. I send this at the risk of my life. There are many more things upon which I could enlighten you, but fear prevents us from doing so, and we trust your Majesty will send us relief as speedily as possible.

God preserve the Royal Person of your Catholic Majesty for many years, as christianity has need of it.

JUAN NUNEZ RIOS.

St. Augustine, Fla., Feb. 19th, 1600.

Sire:

While serving your Majesty in this Garrison of St. Augustine, Florida, as Captain of one of the companies with the title given me by General Menendez Canso, it is the same position my father served previously for a year and a half before the work and place was turned over to me as your Majesty's service required. Later Lieutenant Alvarez Hernando Metas having arrived with certain dispatches regarding my father, who had preceded me, the Governor, without giving any reason or consulting me in any way, has taken the company from me and given it to Lieutenant Metas, who is at present serving. The Governor has only said to me that he wished to employ me in other services of your Majesty for which reason I am detained in this Province on half pay. Although I have asked permission to serve on the Armada and assist in any way I am ordered, as is my duty, he will not allow me to do so, but detains me here. I implore you to send me orders if only to be in the infantry of this Garrison; anything until I am ordered elsewhere, to serve your Majesty. This is my profession and I have always followed it, and for which I shall always hope to receive special encomiums from your Majesty, whom I pray our Lord will bless and protect and preserve from all harm.

       ANTONIO MENENDEZ CANSO.
St. Augustine, Fla., 26th ——, 1600.

Sire:

In other letters I have written to your Majesty I have given an account of the fire we had on the 14th of March of last year, 1599, in this city. Among other houses burned with the church was ours and we came to the hospital for shelter, where we still are, and I implore your Majesty to rebuild our house. The seven hundred ducats required to repair and cover the house which was burned, and which we hope you will send us, will be placed in deposit with the treasurer of this Province until a decision has been reached regarding this country. On account of its ruined and barren condition it is incapable of maintaining so many natives as there are, and as was demonstrated the other day, many seem to think they will order this Garrison removed to another part more advantageous. Should this be the case, your servants will advise you at once of all that occurs.

In the report I give you of the Indians I must say, my Lord, that we make little progress and are but poorly esteemed by them. The fault must lie in us, as there will no doubt be those who will so report it to your Majesty. The good esteem which I am ordered to have for the Governor I shall comply with in every respect except that I shall not lose my rights; these I shall maintain as I have always done. In sending out the Friars to convert and teach the doctrine, I have always observed the order given by your Majesty with the title of Royal Patron. Since it is a truth perfectly well known that no Friar has been sent by me or my predecessors to convert and teach without the permission and sanction of the Governor, and should it become necessary I will so make him confess this truth, which he well knows, as there are so few of us he cannot ignore it, as we eat from his hands at all times. If this country is to be increased and civilized it would be well to send a Bishop here, as it is quite necessary to administer the sacrament of confirmation; therefore, for the peace of those who live here, it would be well for your Majesty to consider and provide as you see fit and God would wish. There is nothing a man can desire more than the salvation of his soul, for this it seems to me urgent that I should retire from this work and take shelter where I can obtain this end, serving in quietude your Majesty. For this I beg and humbly implore your Majesty to send me a permit to go to Spain, as I feel assured of the little success I can obtain by remaining in this country. May our blessed Lord preserve your Majesty in peace and love, Yours,

FRAY BLAS DE MONTES.

St. Augustine, Fla., Feb. 25th, 1600.

Your Lordship:

On the 13th there arrived in this city Diego Ramirez, a citizen of Triana of Sevilla, a second class shipmaster from New Spain, sent by your Viceroy and Royal Officers from San Juan de Ullva. On entering the Bahama channel he was overtaken by a dreadful storm, his vessel sprung a leak and took in so much water they were forced to make for the nearest land which was on the coast of this Province about one hundred and eighty leagues from this city to the north, about thirty-four degrees, more or less, where, on entering a port, the vessel was completely wrecked and the Master made his escape in one of the boats with the papers and dispatches for your Majesty and also some private letters. Coming along the coast, landing at night until he reached the Province of Guale, where last year the Indians had killed two Friars. There he found two vessels in the service of this Garrison which had been sent to carry three or four Casiques, two of them men of great influence in their tribes, who had come to implore mercy for themselves and others for the terrible crime they had committed. I now have them quiet and pacified. These natives carried the master to the ships of this Garrison where he and his men were given shelter and brought to this City.

The natives also gave them what relief they could. On the arrival here of the Master he told me of the dispatches he brought for your Majesty and which he understood were of much importance as they had learned in New Spain that Chinese, English and Flemish were settling there. He asked me for passage for himself and men, for any dispatches I might have for your Majesty and any private mail. He also asked for the means of sustenance from your Royal Treasury, for himself and men, as they had lost all. Considering the importance of the dispatches and papers, and that you might receive them with the utmost speed, I granted their request and also gave them a change of clothes. He did not wish to go to Havana on account of the variable winds and so, as I had a frigate in Port just suitable for the purpose, I fitted it out against the wishes of its owners, to whom I paid the cost of the trip which three pilots assured me would amount to one thousand ducats, not counting the maintenance of the Master and his men. I felt it my duty to aid them from your Royal Treasury, as they were shipwrecked and there was no one in this country who could raise a subscription to supply their wants, all being soldiers or men who have no employment. An account of this may be kept by the judges and officers in Sevilla against this Province. Pedro Redondo Villegas, Auditor of the Artillery of Havana, whom your Majesty nominated to come here to straighten the accounts of this Province, arrived and has commenced his work. He tells me that he is notifying your Majesty of all and calling your attention to some. He says that having notified me of the Royal balance made to Juan Sebadilla, deceased, being as it is, a large sum, it will be well that you send a bill, stating what must be done about its collection. Captain Alonzo de las Alas has not yet satisfied his balance because while investigating his accounts in virtue of the royal decree of appointments and of which he was in charge, was suspended for four years. In accounts taken of different royal officers, they have paid up many losses against your royal estate. I had noticed this and when the accountant Pedro Redondo arrived I suspended these payments until he could look into them and I shall point out to him the result of what I found in them.

On the eighth of February of this year I rendered your Majesty an account of how I sent the collections to your Treasurer, Juan Menendez Marquez. This time the causes made known in the letter which arrived at this Port on the 21st of this month with four vessels and their cargo of provisions, ammunition and money collected from the allowance was too late, so that hereafter your Royal order set forth in Cedule will be obeyed.

This Garrison and territory is at present abounding in the fruits of the earth—corn and other vegetables. Having encouraged and aided in cultivating the land our Lord has seen proper to give us the most fertile year ever known in these Provinces. On the 16th of this month Don Juan, Casique of the Province of San Pedro, died—the one your Majesty was so kind to in sending him two hundred ducats which were given him. I feel his death very much as he was one of the most faithful and influential in this Territory; he was sagacious and practical, having faith, and agreed in all that you ordered. He died as a good christian, receiving the sacraments and giving a good example at the hour of his death to all the Indians and natives. His niece becomes his heir; according to their custom the nieces and nephews become the heirs and not the children.

Fray Baltazar Lopez, of the Franciscan order, has arrived from New Spain. He was crippled and sick, so I gave him permission to go to New Spain where he was cured and has regained his health which has been a great happiness for me as he is greatly needed in the conversion. He has brought many to a realization of the truth of christianity, and I trust in God he

62   *The Unwritten History of*

Land Approach to Fort Marion.

may keep well and continue his good work. In this I try to aid him as much as possible and with some of the officers and soldiers go to visit the Indians from time to time to assure them of our good will and to trade with them. They have just brought from New Spain the five hundred ducats your Majesty gave in charity to the hospital of this City, established for the benefit of the poor soldiers of this Garrison. They also brought five hundred more from Mexico for the Franciscan Convent, and we have also given to said Convent two thousand eight hundred and forty-two reals which were in this Treasury and which were found on the beach of San Mateo from some of the vessels wrecked on that shore, and although your Royal Cedula said it should be three thousand and forty-two reals and a half, the Royal Officers have not been able to find that much on your books, only the amount stated above which was delivered to them for the repairs of the convent. If your Majesty wishes to obtain information regarding Jacon from England you must ask for it by the name of Virginia which is the name given it by the English; if you inquire for Jacon you will get no satisfaction. I send with this a duplicate of the letter written you on February 28th by Pedro Alvarez Castillon via Havana, on the fleet in command of General Sancho Pardo, and as the sea is an uncertain thing I send a duplicate. The frigate which carries this paper and those of the Auditor, Pedro Redondo, belongs to Pedro Gonzales, of Havana, who also goes on her. Should you wish to send dispatches for this Province, Havana or New Spain, this vessel is very appropriate; it is good, small, and sails fast, being of only fifteen tons, and Pedro Gonzales is perfectly familiar with all this coast and is a practical and experienced sailor and can be trusted with anything you wish to send by him. I cannot fail to remind you to grant me a reasonable sum for expenditures of this Garrison, as the expenses are so heavy I am obliged to implore this grace of your Majesty.

May God preserve you in health for the good of christianity. GONZALO MENENDEZ CANSO.

St. Augustine, Fla., June 28th, 1600.

I wrote your Majesty by General Sancho Pardo, giving full and detailed account of how I had arranged matters and placed in office as Auditor of the Custom House, of this City, Pedro Redondo, my son, a person perfectly trustworthy, competent and reliable. I have done everything according to your Majesty's orders. I came to the Province of Florida on the fleet, as you graciously ordered me to investigate the accounts of your Royal Officers and other employees. I arrived in Florida on the 29th of March, presented my commissions, which were accepted by the Governor, Gonzalo Menendez. On the 14th of April, after making all inquiries necessary regarding the accounts, I commenced to investigate, not meeting from the Officers that respect which is shown by the army and navy to your Royal employees. Their books being in such a disordered condition, it will take more time than I calculated to finish these investigations, but I will accomplish them with all possible speed. As I have informed your Majesty through others who the persons are, having to give account and the many and arduous difficulties encountered, there being among auditors, agents and shipmasters, about twenty persons—it will take a longer time to accomplish, although I came quite encouraged and desirous of finishing speedily so as to return to Havana to attend the grand artillery review and take my command. I left town for the term of one year, but find I shall be unable to complete these investigations in that time, as it is impossible to leave them in the muddled condition they are at present. Doctor Juan Gonzales, of the Royal Court of the Indias, has told me he could obtain with the consent of the Governor, a prerogative. I implore your Majesty will send this prerogative and see and notify me as to what I am to do. As I have been here so short a time I cannot inform you of all that you ordered me to investigate. All I can say at present is that there are about two hundred and fifty soldiers in this Garrison; they are good and well drilled and disciplined; that the Governor has planted and under cultivation many acres of land, which will be a great help in the sustenance of these people, who are mostly married, and whose small wages and rations given them does not suffice for their support. They certainly need this grain. Besides others, seeing the good results and what good land it is, are following the example and are clearing and planting fields. With the cutting down of the timber it has done away with the vast quantities of mosquitoes and has helped to improve the City, as one sees on all sides houses in course of construction. The greatest difficulty I find is the difference existing between the Officers of the Royal command and the people. As you have ordered that all should obey them, they are overbearing, as occurs in many other places. If you could devise some remedy for this, all would go well. I shall continue to keep you advised of all that occurs, especially on the matter of investigations and as to who the guilty parties may be. May God grant you a long life of prosperity. FRANCISCO REDONDO VILLEGAS.

St. Augustine, Florida, April 18th, 1600.

CHAPTER VI.

A. D. 1605-1608.

Minutes of a Bull to be presented to the Holy See, asking concession of graces and powers for Catholic residents in Florida—Minorcan families brought a Priest and Monk with them, and wish privileges and new license granted—Instructions as to duties on wine—Priests and Monks of Tasco use municipal monies for their own interests—Advises change in office of Treasurer of the Royal chest—Loss of vessels carrying papers for his Majesty—People of the Kingdom gratified at favor shown by his Majesty to Don Francisco — Letter from Pedro Ibarra to his Majesty—Insufficient support for the Garrison—A widow, who was the wife of two Army Captains, in need—Two poor soldiers find amber in a fish for which Menendez exacted a duty—Anxiety on account of French and English pirates—Some taken prisoners and ten hanged—Several Casiques and chiefs visit Augustine—Are impressed with religious services and procession—Ask for Friars to return to their country with them to instruct their people—Asks for men to assist in building a fort at the mouth of Miguel Moro—Has made inquiry as to origin and source of River San Mateo and Lake Miami—A Garrison of warlike people—Proposition to establish a Manager of the Inquisition to control them—Does not wish to let go certain Priest and Captain — Report of Jaun

Menendez Marquez to the King — Deplores the decision to reduce the Garrison—Advises return to the policy of Pedro Menendez, his cousin—Desires permission to go to Spain to more fully lay the matter before his Majesty.

A. D. 1605.

Minutes of the Bull or Supplication which the Minister of this Court in Rome should present to the Holy See, asking for the concession of new graces and powers in favor of the Catholic residents in Florida, which precepts have been formulated by the Judge complying with the Royal Decree of your Majesty in consultation with the Council.

As formal instructions they should state that these Minorcan families transmigrated to Florida under the English dominion, but with the free use and privilege of their Catholic Religion. They carried with them as spiritual directors Don Pedro Campos, secular Priest, and Padre Bartolome Casanovas, a Monk, that these, for the legitimate discharge of their Ministerial duties, repair to the Holy See, begging they be constituted Pastor of that flock, dispensing them all the powers necessary, that your Holiness benignantly accede to their urgent petition, to grant them different privileges and powers, among others the administering to that Catholic people all the sacraments, even those not Parochial, except confirmation and Orders, extending this privilege for a term of three years when they shall obtain a new license from the superior Prelates or Bishop nearest to Florida. That is what has been done, because I have received a new Cedula from your Majesty ordering that the proceeds of the duties on wine should not be spent on anything but the bringing of water. I cease, satisfied, that before suspending the execution of this Cedula. I shall take time to inform your Majesty that it was necessary for me to avail myself of this money for these purposes. I do not at present send an account, until I can send it finished, that it may not be a work which the Viceroy may consider impossible to accomplish at so small a cost. I beg of your Majesty to consider it. Otherwise I shall obey to the letter this Cedula and I await your reply. Not receiving a reply, I shall take for granted that your Majesty is satisfied. Being so general and important in this Kingdom the practise of other business, and there being a possibility of misunderstanding in this matter, I resolved to visit some of the vineyards of this kingdom, and so I went to Tasco, some twenty-eight leagues from this city, taking advantage of the Christmas holidays, not to lose any time from my ordinary business, it has been of great advantage as I can state just how these things are conducted. I have stated to your Majesty in other letters, the municipality of this City is not governed as it should be, because the Priests or Monks think more of their own interests, reducing all to their own profit. As this takes place the Royal Officers cannot ordinarily attend the meetings, it would be well that the Viceroy should elect four persons of the best standing and principles upon whom your Majesty should bestow Government offices and that the Viceroy should oblige them to accept, for at least four months in the year, giving them precedence after the Royal Officers, and thus assure their attention to matters which are looked upon indifferently in one of the best Cities you possess, and which is improving each day. If the Council will consider this proposition and your Majesty pleases to execute it.

The Decree sent by me and the Official documents for the high notaries of Government and legislative bodies of this Audience and particularly for the notaries of the Treasury, that they might transact some important business which was taken from the books and have been badly attended to because there is no one to be solicitous about this matter, and it not belonging to the duties of the Judge, it is neglected as are other affairs. It becomes obligatory to find some faithful and trustworthy person of influence to take charge of this Office and assign them a salary of $800.00 a year. Show and make them understand the anxiety which I feel concerning it and how it retards other business. Being new in my Office I have not cared to assign any one until I had a license from your Majesty for doing so. I shall await your decision. It seems to me the salary could be assigned through the Legislature, and if they neglect their duties discharge them.

In New Vera Cruz, Pedro Casco Calderon has been serving as Treasurer of the Royal Chest by nomination of your Majesty, he also occupied other Offices in Spain. He is old, the many years of service at that Post and the conduct of his wife, have disturbed his mind; he is also running a butcher shop and other enterprises not in accordance with the Royal Office. The situation is such that nothing should be concealed from you. In being served you might give him some small Office at home, and I should remove him to some other place, if I did not understand the necessity of his attending to his estate, which is in that neighborhood, and all his other profitable enterprises.

The first registered vessel was lost on the coast of Campeachy, and although the Papers for your Majesty were taken out, they had been under water so long that they were useless, scarcely legible. The second vessel of advice was taken by the French on its return from Saona, and they stripped it of everything, leaving vessel and crew in such a ruined condition they could proceed no further than Santo Domingo. Seeing that they were lost they threw the papers for your Majesty overboard. Thus it becomes necessary that one and the other be duplicated. Your Majesty will please see that the person in Sevilla who has charge of these vessels be careful of the person to whom he entrusts these Documents as so far the person in charge does not seem to understand their importance, and so, it is only miraculous that we get them at all. It has been very gratifying to all in this Kingdom the favor shown by your Majesty to Don Francisco. I trust he will serve you well and faithfully. It is prohibited that an Alderman should serve a private individual under penalty of losing his Office. In this city Don Luis Maldona, son of Maldona who was Judge of this Supreme Court, has a regiment. On account of his talent and the good services he can render I have him occupied in my service, and that he may not fall under the penalty of the law I implore your Majesty to send him a permit that he may attend to both, or a license that he may resign his place in the regiment and serve your Majesty otherwise, on a salary that you shall name. I consider the first plan best. Don Luis Valasco has arrived and

I thought best to introduce him and have some attention bestowed upon him, on account of his position. I shall show him all respect and visit him, feeling sure you will thus be well served. The case is free of consequences. Having sent you a letter of dispatch through the Supreme Court of Castile stating that Dr. Lievana will go over to that Kingdom and render an account of the expenses of the residence and trip of the first Lieutenant of Assistencia of Sevilla. Dr. Lievana acted as Mayor in the interim between the death of Senor Trufillo and your appointing Don Francisco de Onate. He is a person who will render you good service, he can be relied on, is among the noblest here, and could fill any office. I have detained this vessel that I might inform you of the departure of the vessel for the Phillipines.

May God preserve you for many years.

THE MARQUEZ OF MONTES CLARAS.

Mexico, March 31st, 1605.

(There is a Rubrica.)

Sire: A. D. 1605.

I sent your Majesty one of your royal Cedulas dated in Valladolid, April 3rd, in which I laid before your Majesty the necessity and want these poor married men are in. It is impossible for them to support themselves; there are seven and eight in a family to be fed on the father's rations. As I have before stated to you, it would be a great charity as well as a service to God to help them that they may not perish. This may be remedied when the other people arrive. I can then give permission to the valetudinarians and sick to return home, your Majesty having sent as a reward for so many years of service the means to defray the cost of the voyage. I can give according to the condition of each one and to the married men who remain here in service please order an extra half ration for each child with some other slight assistance while they serve as soldiers and their daughters are too young to marry. I assure you that aside from being a great charity it will be no more than justice, as they are among the best soldiers I have ever seen on land or sea. Among the necessities your Majesty may see proper to relieve is the suffering of a lady of standing, widow of two captains who served many years in this Province and who had charge of it in the absence of the Governors. Aid given here will be one of the greatest of charities, as before stated. The negroes who were here for over forty years, working in the Havana forces, have died, and it will be well to send about a dozen more and three or four negro women.

Your order that I should not collect from the New Spain more than was necessary I have carried out so far, and I wish to remind you to send a trustworthy accountant as the one at present occupying that office is not fitted for it. During the residence of Gonzalo Menendez Canso, the Treasurer, Juan Menendez, asked and exacted that duty should be paid your Majesty on some amber which Bartolaine Perez and Gaspar Martin, soldiers, had found in a fish's craw, and with promises which Gonzalo Menendez made the soldiers, he palliated them and said the duty must be paid according to one of the chapters of royal instruction. At that time we could not ascertain if it were true. The said soldiers had already put in a plea to the said Gonzalo Menendez and as interested parties could not be witnesses in these investigations. The other person through whose hands it must pass was Lieutenant Fabeicio Lopez, and he was not here. He has returned now and makes the accompanying declaration, which you can place with the declaration of the soldiers, and you can have your duties and give the soldiers what was taken from them, not allowing them to make a manifestation. The Treasurer has asked me to let him use a permit he has to go to that kingdom on business and solicitations. I have not allowed him to use it, because we are so much in need of men and there are so few I can put my hand on in case of need. God protect your Majesty.

PEDRO IBARRA.

Dec. 26th, 1605, St. Augustine, Florida.

Sire: A. D. 1607.

In a letter of the 22nd of January of the present year, which was sent from Havana with a notice of the death of Governor Don Pedro Acuna I have forwarded you, I have also notified you of what I thought of doing with the French and English pirates I held as prisoners. One day after the departure of the boat I sent to have them hanged, using with them such religious treatment as is customary. Ten of them were baptized, the others stated they had already been baptized. It seems that all died as Christians, so that this whole City with their fraternities turned out to lay them out and bury them. I only wish that with

Old St. Augustine

these pirates we might put an end to them all on these coasts. There are so many they keep me in great anxiety and I implore you to send me people to destroy them. I have every one on this coast enlisted to aid in their destruction. But my experience is that many have not only sheltered them, saved their lives and estates, but continue to serve them and allow them to come and go at will. They come from a distance of a hundred leagues with all confidence and safety. This week, which is Holy week, I have had here several Casiques and Chiefs who are the lords of the mouth of Miguel Mora, where, I have before told you, we should erect a fort and from there capture the fleet of Charles. I shall tell you the names of these Casiques that you may know who they are and the great achievement I have made in gaining their services. They have returned to their country dressed and very happy and edified with the religious services and processions they have witnessed during this Holy season. They ask for Friars to instruct them. I told them I would come there to visit them. I notify you that this is the time that with more security and less cost a fort could be built there; they themselves would act as peons, and if possible to do so I would myself ask that from Havana they would send me an engineer and eighty men with two launches. Look into this, as I am quite sure they would all lend themselves to serve in the building, as they would feel safe all along that coast from the invasions of the enemy. The other Provinces are very peaceful. With the warriors, silver miners and woodmen I have so long asked your Majesty to send me, I trust in God that we can touch with our hands the great wealth we surely have in the interior of this land. All this I ask of you I am moved to do by the zeal to serve you and enlarge your estate and not for rest or gain. From all these parts I have had here this week over five hundred Indians, and, God knows, to make them understand it, will require more men than I have in our Order to guide them.

In a letter of September 23rd your Majesty commands me to make every possible inquiry to know the origin and source of the River San Mateo and Lake Miami. As I have always tried to make inquiries, about six months ago I discovered on the southern coast a river which I have had examined by three different pilots, and find that it has nine fathoms of water at the entrance of a much wider river. I notified your Majesty of this new river. This garrison is composed of a warlike people and the Friars of San Francisco are thinking of establishing a Manager of the Inquisition to subject them and control their passions. When I came here these warriors were in great want and I have come to an agreement together with the Royal Officers, that we should have Juan Nunez go to Castilla and try to make terms with some merchant to remedy these occurrences. To Fray Pedro Ruiz they have brought an Order from your Majesty in which you command me to let him go to Castilla on account of his age and failing health; that he is of no further use. It seems to me this Friar has not been here so many years and he is perfectly sound and fresh and robust, never having had so much as a headache.

Captain Alonzo de las Alas has presented me a Cedula from your Majesty which gives him permission to go to Castilla for a term of two years and that during that time he is to receive no salary. He claims that it is an oversight in not appointing some one in his place and allowing him to draw his salary as heretofore and which is just, because whoever takes his place is entitled to half of his pay, and for this it will be necessary that your Majesty order Bartolome Arruchas to return to his Post as the permit granted him by your Majesty has expired.

God protect your Majesty. PEDRO IBARRA.
May 16th, 1607, St. Augustine, Fla.

Your Lordship: A. D. 1608.

Through a letter of September 20th of last year, 1602, and an account rendered the Bishop of Cuba (the past year of 1606) who came to confirm the Spanish Christians not yet confirmed and the native Indians of these Provinces, I told him all that I thought would be most convenient to the service of God our Lord and your Majesty regarding the conversion of this Garrison to which I again refer, it having come to my knowledge that your Royal Council did not repeat it to you, fearing to tire or annoy you. Now, on learning the resolution you have taken of reforming this Garrison and reducing it to one hundred and fifty infantry, I am sure you have listened to the advice of persons who have never seen this coast, nor do they know anything about the interior of the country. nor the great benefits which have been accomplished in the conversion of the natives who are idolaters and savages, hesitating at no crime however horrible.

If Gonzalo Menendez Canso were moved with the true zeal of God and a proper desire to serve your Majesty it would have been no more than just that when he first assumed control of this Government he should have given you a full and detailed account of the existing state of affairs and sought your advice and not waited until he was quite sure that his Office was to be filled by some one else.

Again, I decided to write this to implore you to consider and look closely into the matters upon which I have advised you and which I have done in all truth and fidelity as I am obliged to for my King. Knowing also that the King of glorious memory, your father, had more trouble and combats than at present on account of economy and the abandoning of this Garrison, he never listened to such things; on the contrary, in the time of Governor General Pedro Menendez Marquez, my first cousin, he increased the force to one hundred and fifty soldiers of Infantry and by thus assigning them to this Post their aid and succor succeeded in subjugating the Indians and in bringing and attracting them to hear the Holy Gospel, and listen to the words of the Friars who preached. This is a public truth. And since that time no Governor has made any conquests or discoveries, nor gone in person to treat with the Indians nor draw them towards civilization by gifts or other means. And if you would at least grant us a Garrison of defense of three hundred Infantry and thirty marines besides the Friars, Governor and Royal officials, with orders that they proceed to feret out the secrets of the interior of the country, where Lieutenant Mocana entered, and in which latitude there can no doubt be found an excellent port, particularly at Cayagua, where any Armada could with safety enter in an altitude of thirty-three and one-fourth degrees, and where I have myself been in the past year of 1588. Should it prove advantageous and convenient in the Bay of the Mother of God, of Macan, at a height of thirty-seven degrees at its mouth, and which terminates at the foot of the mountain range where I was also, in the same year, in search of the English settlement. It is a more sheltered harbor than this one and nearer for obtaining aid, and an entrance could be made through the Province of Guale in the land of Tulufino, which corresponds with that called Tama, on the skirts of the mountain range. It might be a very advantageous move which would result in the glory of God and your Majesty's interest; for if we could bring these people to honor the Governor of the garrison and when they found that he was working for their good and not the contrary, there would naturally result a reform among the enemies and we might aspire to carry out your designs in a satisfactory manner. Under existing circumstances it is impossible for this Garrison, composed of so few men, to march out or in any way try to defend themselves against the enemy, and nothing remains but to die bravely defending the Garrison as best they can, and when there remains no one else to defend it, it leaves the Friars and converted Indians to the mercy of God, for it is the only help they can look to, the Forts and Castles of Flanders being so far away they would be slow to respond. If there is to be no more infantry sent I think it would be well to agree upon making this Fort a ravelin and build a good trench of defense along the coast to prevent the enemy from jumping over and in every possible way attend to the preservation of all the above mentioned regarding the Friars and converted natives. Put a stop to all these ambushes and skirmishes and other nuisances which oblige them (the natives) to leave their settlements and fortify themselves upon your domains and do great damage to vessels coming in and going out at the mouth of the Bahama channel, making it unsafe all along the coast of this part of the Indies, possessed by your Majesty and which you will possess for many years for the glory of God and the welfare of the souls of these poor natives, and may His Divine Majesty not permit these arbitrations and troubles caused by a few men who are incited by their passions and own selfish interests and with the pretext of saving you some twenty or thirty thousand dollars cause such great trouble that your expenses will be more than doubled in repairing the damage. You support and maintain the Garrisons of Havana and Porto Rico from rents and taxes of New Spain and it is not just nor proper to put difficulties in your way to prevent you from preserving and sustaining in the same way this one which should be well defended as it is a Port from whence you can pass through those same inland regions to Mexico, and, in my opinion, it is very important to preserve it for this purpose. Havana is of importance, being the key to the Indias and a place where the Armadas and fleets can replenish and repair to continue their voyages through these Kingdoms. With all humility I beg you receive my zeal and good wishes which is to always serve you with fidelity and truth as has been done by my parents, and if on this occasion I did not call your attention to these matters, which are of vast import, I should be committing a crime, and in all this I subject myself to better judgment and implore your Majesty with all humility that as I can be of no other use in this Post, but to serve as Treasurer of these Provinces, which I am at present doing, you will consider my application and give me permission to go to Spain and render an account of the Royal finances intrusted to my care since June of the past year of 1602, hereafter and for this purpose that I be given receipts of my charge, and that during my absence from this Port the employment be at the risk and account of the person left in my place, and who must give bond as is customary in vacations of similar Posts and offices and at the same time that the Governor provide that he be given one half of the salary and that I receive the other half as a means of helping me to defray my expenses. and if my mind does not deceive me my services are deserving of it for the care and anxiety I have suffered in this Garrison by wishing to defend the cause of the profit of the Royal finance of your Majesty and the desire that I have of settling my accounts, not only those I have of my own, but also those of Pedro Redondo which will seem to have been given with pay, which will be the case with those I render if God will give me life for it to employ in your Royal Service. May God grant you many and happy years for the mercy and defense of the faith, the preservation of peace and tranquility of many more kingdoms, and the conversion of as many idolaters as are in these parts. JUAN MENENDEZ MARQUEZ.

St. Augustine, Fla., January 5th, 1608.

CHAPTER VII.

A. D. 1622-1640.

Report of Antonio Benavides to his Majesty — Endeavored to execute order of the King to establish friendly relations with the English of the Carolinas —Sent Don Francisco Menendez together with other Officers—The Mission a failure owing to the English not having instruction from London— Find that the English have built fort on Spanish territory—Requested its removal in order to avoid trouble between the two nations — The English Governor refused—Matter fully laid before his Majesty—Report of Luis De Rojas—Frigate sent from Augustine to Havana to help fleet from New Spain bring over supplies for Garrison — They discover thirteen vessels, which proves to be an enemy who give chase to the Frigate—The pilot and soldiers landed, followed by the enemy, until a forest is reached, where the enemy leaves them —Returning to their launches the enemy strip the Frigate and burn the hull—The enemy coast along shore frightening the Indians, lodging in their huts —A large force of Indians were gathered together with one hundred and fifty soldiers to pursue the enemy at which they reembark and sail away— A Spanish Frigate arrives bearing forty-seven persons, all that was left of three vessels which had been captured by the enemy who proved to be bearing provisions to a Dutch Fleet in Havana—

Old St. Augustine 83

Recommends his Majesty to build a fort at the Bar at the place called Jega—Report of Luis Ussitinez to his Majesty—The Mandate of the King has been carried out in regard to prayer to God for the success of the King's arms taken up against France— 1636—An account of a meeting of the Board of the City Council of Havana at which a clergyman of the Holy Office of the Inquisition appears with an Auto from the Senior Commissionado, Don Francisco de las Casas, of the Holy Office of this city, containing instructions as to certain ceremonies in connection with the Inquisition.

Your Lordship:

By your Royal dispatch of last year you ordered me to immediately establish friendly relations with the English of the Carolinas, and that your Majesty had asked that the Court of London should pass efficacious measures to have the order repeated, which was given in virtue of the suspension of arms between your Majesty's crown and that of England, to the end that these vessels be not disturbed by the English of the Carolinas, nor the Indians of their Province, so that they may derive the benefits of the land and live in tranquility and love as your Majesty desires. That for this purpose I should in my ministerial capacity go to the Governor of Carolina instigating him to make them observe punctually the treaty of suspension of arms. I executed this order immediately and sent the Auditor Don Francisco Menendez accompanied by other Officers of the Garrison of this Post, with orders to adjust a firm agreement with the Governor that on the part of the English they should cease to incite the Indians, and thus they and the laborers might live without injury one from the other; that this agreement was equally important for both Nations. To this proposition, and others certified, in the testimony of the letter which the referred to Don Francisco Menendez carried and on this occasion I remit to you. The Governor and parliament of the Carolina replied that they had received no orders from the King of Great Britain, but that notwithstanding they would try to maintain friendly relations with this Government during the suspension of arms. Immediately upon the arrival of Auditor Don Francisco Menendez in Carolina, he was informed that the English had built a wooden fort at the mouth of Talaje, one of your Provinces, where for many years were settled the Indians, and on account of the blockade we put upon it, they retired. Don Francisco immediately demanded of the Governor and Parliament the reason for building there; that it was your Majesty's Territory, etc., and stating that it might cause trouble between the two Nations and once that war was started it would be difficult to stop on account of the Indians. His reply was simply that to secure his dominions from invasion and harm, the King of Great Britain had ordered it built, and that they should found Towns in the best and most approved manner. The Auditor requested its removal from your Territory, but they refused to do so, stating that his orders were not sufficient, and expressed nothing whatever in regard to this Fort. I infer that with the incoming of this new Governor in the Carolinas, not only will the Fort be completed, but they will settle all the Islands belonging to your jurisdiction, and thus make the Carolinas im-

Old St. Augustine 85

pregnable and reduce this Garrison to a more lamentable condition than it is, and the Indians watching their opportunities will come upon us and also takes sides with the English, who will supply them with arms and ammunition, a thing they most ardently desire. The Auditor was also informed that in the Carolinas they were waiting the arrival of large quantities of arms and ammunition from England. They can in time of war easily invade this Castle, the only desire and aim they have, on account of the great importance it would be to the preservation of their colonies in this New England and the facility it would give them for capturing vessels coming and going through the Bahama Channel, the nearness of this Castle being just what they most desire. In giving you this information I not only appease my conscience but fulfilled my obligations to you by showing you the great danger which threatens you and the terrible results it might cause, and I leave it to the intelligence of your Royal Highness to act in this matter as best pleases you.

May God save you. ANTONIO BENAVIDES.

St. Augustine, Fla., April 21st, 1622.

Sire: 1627.

After having written your Majesty giving an account of having faithfully fulfilled all the instructions of your different Royal Cedula, I will, in this, give a detailed account of what occurred on August 25th of this year. I ordered Captain Diego del Pozo to embark in one of the frigates of your Majesty's Service in this Garrison, and proceed to Havana, to help bring over the supply for this Garrison, which was to come on the fleet from New Spain. Following his journey and coasting along these Provinces, near the Cape of Canaveral, on Sunday, the 13th of September, in the morning, he discovered thirteen vessels, ten large ones and three smaller ones. Believing it to be the Fleet, he made signals and hoisted the flag, but as no answer was returned he saw clearly that it was the enemy. At the same time one of their three smaller vessels came forward and gave him chase. The Frigate being small went so near in shore that the vessel could not reach it, seeing which they lowered two rowboats to chase and attack the Frigate, each boat carrying twelve- soldiers and ten mariners. The Frigate resisted the attack with arquebuses. The enemy not making any headway, called for more aid, which was sent them by two more larger launches with a hundred men. Captain Diego del Pozo finding himself in such a tight place, and the pilot and soldiers thinking they would stand a better chance on land, he decided to land. The enemy followed close, he fought them step by step until they came to a thick forest, when the enemy decided to leave them. The skirmish lasted about two hours. On returning to their launches the enemy first stripped the Frigate of all they wanted and burned the hull. When Captain Pozo saw that he would have to abandon the ship, he threw the two pieces of artillery he carried overboard. All this occurred about forty leagues from this Garrison. In a few days I was notified of this misfortune and I sent a launch with infantry to get the men from the Frigate. All arrived safely without the loss of a single man. I had the testimony taken and ascertained the truth and found that the Captain and his men were here and did their duty faithfully. Further proof and truth was ascertained a few days later from the soldiers I sent by land to reconnoitre the coast where the Frigate was lost—they brought word that the thirteen vessels which had been sent to chase the Frigate were coasting along slowly taking on water and wood. They had disembarked and taken up lodging in the Indian huts, the Indians fleeing with fear. Some, by gifts, had been induced to return, others came to me for protection. Following this, I received further news that three of the thirteen vessels were lost and the crew on land. This proved not to be true—in going over the Bar three launches were lost and a few of the men drowned. Feeling it was not right to have the enemy land on your Majesty's domain, where we are at present safe and on friendly relations with the Indians, I immediately gave orders and gathered a large force of Indians and, with a hundred and fifty of our men, I set out determined to find the enemy and thrust them out. I appointed Captain Melchar Durante to take command here during my absence, he being an old man of much experience. I was continuing my pursuit of the enemy when I received news of their having re-embarked and sailed off, so I returned sending one of the Sergeants with a squad of twenty men to the Bar, and that they might recover the three launches if they were worth it. This they did promptly, returning with two of the launches in fair condition, the third they left as it was too badly injured to be of use. They brought the same news of the enemy's proceedings. On the 20th of said month a Frigate arrived. On sending out to recognize her, we found it to be Spanish. It was one of the fleet which was overtaken by the enemy and brought in forty-seven persons, mariners and passengers, among them an Augustinian Monk. It was what was left of the three vessels taken by the enemy of the thirteen vessels. They were captured off Cape San Antonio. On one of the vessels were the papers and information sent by the Viceroy to Don Carlos Ybarra, General of the Spanish fleet, which was coming from Spain. They captured it near Cape Catoche, and the papers for General Ybarra and your Majesty were thrown overboard to prevent the enemy from getting them. They were in the enemy's power for twelve days, when they put them on this small Frigate with scant rations, and told them they were free to come to this Garrison, where they arrived half-starved. I took them in and fed them at your Majesty's expense, as part of them had lost their lives in your service and they were your vassals. They remained here a month, and on the first opportunity which presented itself, I gave them passage for Havana. Among the forty-six persons were four pilots and four boatswain who gave a long account of what they heard while prisoners. They particularly spoke of the Armada in charge of Tomas Raspuro, which they had been waiting for, but on seeing so many large vessels of war and knowing they would be outnumbered, they desisted and retired along the coast—it was then they captured these three frigates of this Garrison of which I have given you detailed account. These Pilots informed me that these thirteen vessels came with supplies and ammunition and provisions for the Dutch fleet, which was in Havana, but they learned it had departed and they were too late. Being unable to assault our Fleet as she entered the mouth of the channel, they decided to take one of the Pilots who was experienced in the Honduras waters and there await the Admiral and Captain of our fleet and make them prisoners. They questioned them the whole time they were prisoners and asked their advice, finally turning them loose on the small frigate, so that it was a miracle they were saved. The thirteen vessels were manned by very young men, most of them boys, and they could not tell the name of the squadron, but the Admiral was Pedro Yanez, a German, a native of Amsterdam. They got all the information possible regarding this Garrison, and say that next summer they will come and ransack and burn the City. At that time there were only forty men, less than the three hudred you should always maintain here—so, I selected others, forced them into service and have them drilled and armed. I have given you a full account of all the happenings on the coast this summer. I hope I have done so, as a good vassal, and for this reason I should warn and advise your Majesty to build a Fort at the Bar at a place they call Jega—it being the place where vessels all come to cast anchor when they want to take on water, wood, and to await the merchant ships and others they wish to capture. Many of your ships and nearly all those bringing supplies to this Garrison are lost in this way. A Fort at this place would act as a sentinel, and guard against their landing and helping themselves. It would also be well to have it in case of vessels being wrecked along this coast, as so many are, to be able to rescue and save the crews and passengers, who so often perish at the hands of pirates and cruel Indians. One cannot trust the Indians, they are children born of traitors. I am sure the Germans would not approach if they saw the place occupied by Spaniards. For this you would be obliged to increase a hundred soldiers more than are in this Garrison. Besides the men would have to be relieved from time to time from there as the work would be arduous, and no soldier or any one could withstand the mosquitoes which are so bad they kill the men, and destroy much of the food. The cost of this Fort you would have to send some one to estimate. I could not feel that I had properly complied with my duty until I have notified you of this great and urgent need. Hoping your Majesty may spend many happy years, as your vassals need you.

LUIS DE ROJAS.

St. Augustine, Fla., February 13th, 1627.

Sire: A. D. 1636.

By a Cedula of your Royal Highness, dated in Madrid, on the 28th of June of last year, you command me to have a general offering of prayer in all the churches in the district under my command, imploring God that you may be successful in the arms you have taken up against France, on account of her evil designs against you. You also recommend that I improve the conduct and manners of the people here; that if necessary I punish them publicly for their offences. I immediately complied with your order, and had them go out from the high church in procession, those of the Seraphic Order joining with all the others. They went through all the streets of the City, then a high mass was sung, and prayers offered for

your success. I also sent a message to all the other Churches and Convents to have like services celebrated. In regard to the conduct of the residents of these Province, Spaniards as well as natives, I have great care in every respect, and from today, complying with your Mandate, I shall redouble my vigilance. May God spare your Majesty many years, for the good of Christianity. LUIS USSITINEZ.
St. Augustine, Fla.

Havana, A. D. 1640.

In the city of Havana on the 13th day of April, 1678, there was a meeting of the Board in the Hall of the City Council as is usual and customary. The Master of the Field, Don Francisco Davila, Governor and Captain-General of said City, and the Messrs. Nicolas Castellan, Lieutenant-Major Don Pedro Valdes, Don Pedro Recio de Oquendo, First Alderman, Captain Don Blas Pedraso.

In the presence of the Notary, the following was agreed:

They had begun to discuss some business when there was a rap at the door, the Governor rang the bell, the porter opened the door and said that outside was the Lieutenant Don Antonio Grazeano, a noted clergyman of the Holy Office of the Inquisition, that he brought a message from the Inquisition for his Lordship of the Board. He sent this youngest Alderman with the Secretary to receive him, as he came in the name of the Inquisition. Entering and having been seated in the midst of the Aldermen, he announced that he brought an Auto from the Senor Comissionado, Don Francisco de las Casas, of the Holy Office of this City. He was told to read it, which he did, and delivered it. His Lordship asked that he give testimony of his authority in order to agree upon the matter of which it treated, and for the better veneration of God and of so Holy a Tribunal. Don Antonio Glaziano drew forth from his pocket a folded paper which he delivered in my, the Notary's' presence. Opening it, it contained a sheet of paper, the first leaf of which was written on both sides, signed, it appeared, by the said Don Antonio Graziano. This duty performed, he arose and left, accompanying him to the door, the same ones who received him, and I, the present Notary. The door being closed his Lordship ordered inserted to the letter the testimony, the tenor of which is as follows:

In the City of Havana on the same day, Dr. Francisco de las Casas, "Comissionado" of the Holy Office of the Inquisition in the City of Carthagena, said: That last Sunday, the eighth of the current month, seeming to him opportune, and by order of the Holy Tribunal for which purpose he warned and made known to the present Notary and all the gentlemen of the Board, that they might concur to their duty as ordered by your Majesty, preceding these courtesies and compliments.

That on the day appointed they should go from the residence of the Lord Comissionado to the Holy Parochial Church of this City, in the order referred in the testimony given by the present Notary. The function terminated, they should leave the church, return to the residence of the Lord Comissionado. It seems they wished to alter this form at the gates and places

they had been, and, as on the day of the Anethema the
same celebration must be repeated, the Lord Comissionado wished, with the best intentions, and not to
be lacking in the form observed by the Tribunal for
said act to which they should cling, this was entirely
for the reasons of his Office and to avoid public altercations, from which originate unnecessary noise and
unrest, contrary to the decency and gravity of this
Tribunal. This is well known to the Tribunal and
Board of said City, it must be done in the following
manner: That the Board should come in this form to
the residence of the Lord Commissionado and conduct
him to the church, he going by the side of the Governor, the other ministers each one between two Aldermen, according to the Office and time of service and
somewhat in advance of this Lord Commissionado
and Governor with the standard of the Faith which
must be carried by the person of greatest authority
who should be present. The balls of the standard by
the next in authority. That on arriving at the church
the priests must come out to receive them, sprinkling
them with holy water, and conduct them to their seats,
which shall be in the High Chapel, on the Gospel side.
in a chair covered with velvet and a carpet at the
feet. Consecutively, next to the Governor and Lord
Commissionado on a covered bench, the High Constable and other attendants and ministers of the Holy
Office. That the Governor and Board are to be seated
thus the day of publication, on the Gospel side; that
the Lord Commissionado should be the preferred in
all things; that at the hour for leaving, the Notary accompanied by two attendants, will mount the pulpit
and from thence he shall swear them in, in a loud voice,

to the oath of Faith. This finished, they are to take the Lord Commissionado back to his residence. They are to try and carry out these ceremonies in as grave and reverential a manner as possible, this being one of the most important ceremonies of the Holy Office of the Inquisition, and this City belongs to its District. There are reasons for other ceremonies, and so I, the present Notary, was ordered to witness them, that I might give testimony and the work proceed according to the acts published, and so that all could be reported to the Lord Inquisitadores of the Holy Tribunal. Then it was provided and ordered to be signed.

DR. FRANCISCO DE LAS CASAS.

This agrees with the original which I have in my possession, and having consulted the matter, the following was agreed upon:

First: As regards the form in which the City, according to the acts of Faith, must proceed to the Residence of the Lord Commissionado and Minister of the Holy Office, as also in the public streets, we cite or quote a Cedula from your Majesty where you refer to Don Juan Solozano, whose political authority in Peru entitles him to have a voice, and on this point we are warned by your Majesty to guard against the Lord Commissionado assuming superiority of the Governor. In Peru, where the matter was first discussed of precedence the form is as follows: The City goes from the City Hall, as customary, to the residence of the Lord Commissionado, where he is awaiting them in the yard. There he is incorporated in the procession, being placed at the left of the Governor, and all march in twos, the magistrates and constables of longest

Old St. Augustine 95

standing given the preference, and the Ministers of the Holy Office intermixed, but preference always to the Officers of Justice. On arriving at the church, assigning seats and all through the ceremonies care is taken that the greatest preference and respect be shown the Governor, as stated in your Royal Cedula, and thus it was conducted last Sunday in going and coming from which much discussion has arisen, as certified in the testimony which I, the present Notary, insert to the letter, although the Lord Commissionado states in the Auto that all preference was given the Governor. 1640.

CHAPTER VIII.

A. D. 1655-1657.

An anonymous letter to his Majesty recounts the death of Governor Benito Ruid Salazer by a contagious sickness during the absence of the Sergeant Major —The office is held by two others pro tem.—They also died suddenly after serving a short term— Certain officials of the Garrison who are related meet at night and elect as Governor Don Pedro Ruitinez—Who intimidates the people and squanders the money sent for their support—The Treasurer a partner in the illegality, and the Judge receives hush money—This Governor maltreated an official who is also a soldier and a conveyor of monies and goods for this port from Havana, for his Majesty—Traffic in amber from the Indians— Taking the iron and implements sent to be used in repairing the Fort as money to purchase this amber —Declares he will consult his own pleasure concerning the laws of the Church, taking communion once in one and one-half years—A distressing condition of mismanagement—No name signed to the letter—A report from Diego Robelledo, 1657, concerning the necessity of having an officer to guard the port for incoming and outgoing vessels as pirates had frequently entered and landed before notice could be given—Also the appointment of an officer and twelve infantrymen to guard other ports of the coast—He desists from building more

Old St. Augustine 97

fortifications because of the opposition of the Friars, who protested that the proximity of the Spaniards would retard the conversion of the Indians— The Governor feels that the danger is far greater to the development of his Majesty's Provinces to allow the enemy a foothold in a Province as rich as Appalachicola—The great distance of some of the Provinces—Indians dying with smallpox—The burden of carrying food such a distance on the shoulders of men — Fray Jaun Gomez reports (1657) of the uprising of some of the Indian Chiefs who march to St. Augustine and hang the Governor because of his insistance on their carrying heavy loads of corn into the settlement, when they, the Indians, had vassals to perform such labors— Reports that the Island of Jamaica is heavily fortified by the English who intend taking Cuba— These reports causing much uneasiness in these Provinces.

My Lord: A. D. 1655.

Moved by piety, and a desire for peace and quietude, it has seemed to me timely to notify you regarding the Government of this Province and Garrison of St. Augustine, Fla., being as you are so high and compassionate a Minister, who is always thinking and caring for the welfare of his people. My Lord, Governor Benito Ruid Salazar, former Governor of this Province, died at the time the Sergeant-Major was absent. God, it seems, took him by a contageous sickness, and although two others have been nominated *pro tem.*, by the death of Benito Ruiz, the reins of government were left in charge of the Auditor Nicolas Ponce de

Leon, who governed for six months more or less, when he died suddenly. For this reason, a few of the Officials of this Garrison, who are related, met at night in different parts of the City, and with sufficient defamatory speech elected as Governor Don Pedro Ruitinez, with flattering promises to those who would give their vote. When he had been Governor one year and a half, he had given twenty-three patents of captain, the most of them to two companies of this Garrison, four positions as wardens of the Fort, three Sergeant-Majors said to be andantes — three Auditors, one Treasurer — calling himself Governor and Captain-General. In granting these patents, and other things he has done, he has thrown down the flags, and had the artillery at the Fort salute. He arrived here on the seventeenth of July, with the Auditor, Treasurer, Sergeant-Major and the two captains of infantry who all left that court at the same time. The Sergeant-Major brought a Cedula from your Majesty, for the Governor, which he presented to Don Pedro Ruitinez, and it was not possible to comply with it, it being a military promotion, placing the Sergeant-Major as Governor. Don Pedro Ruitinez had received notice that Don Diego de Rolallado had been appointed Governor and Captain-General of this Port—he sent some friends over to Havana to meet and entertain him during his stay in that City, and thus Don Pedro has maintained his friendly relations with the Governor, although he has not said a word of how he intimidated the people to elect him Governor—nor his other doings—nor how he refused to turn over the Government to the Sergeant-Major. But he did demand his pay. Your Lordship, the Governor and Captain-General arrived

Old St. Augustine 99

at this Garrison on the 18th of June, 1654, having received in Havana $20,000 sent by the Auditor and placed to the credit of this Garrison. This money he used in Havana as follows: Goods—$7,000, gaining in this purchase more than 200 per cent. He sent Don Alonzo Menendez with $8,000 to relieve the suffering and need of the infantry and others who are in your service, and he sold to advantage the remaining goods. In the month of February of this present year there arrived a vessel laden with flour, iron implements and other goods, and although it is true that the person in whose charge they came, brought over $40,000 to be delivered to this treasury, he only delivered $15,000, because in Havana the duties were so heavy and they demanded the pay. The soldier in whose care this money and goods came, is Domingo Nunez. He spent in Havana $2,000 on clothing, filling an order received from the Governor, and another $2,000 in clothing he was to bring from New Spain. The Governor after ordering this became infuriated with Domingo Nunez, cursing him, beating and slapping him in the most unheard of manner—accusing him of not bringing all the clothing ordered, and finally he had him placed in the stockade on the beach. He then had the boxes and packages taken to a neighbor's and soldier, and opened them—finding after pricing them and adding one-fourth more than the cost to them, that they amounted to more than the $2.000. He then went several times to Domingo Nunez, demanded his papers, searched them, kept him in prison, and then without cause or reason turned him out. It is true he becomes enraged for the slightest cause. It is a positive fact, that he and another spendthrift named Fanfan, have sent out from his (the Governor's) house, chocolate to be sold on the streets by his body guards. At the time there was such great distress and scarcity, he sent out wine to be sold at such exhorbitant prices that only those compelled to have it could buy. In this tavern of his, the people sell cutlasses for bread, chocolate and tobacco. In the large store, run now by Lorenzo Josi, they sell rum and clothing—a bottle of rum costs eight dollars which is an outrage. According to Manuel Barrios, the tavern keeper, he makes thirty-one dollars on a cask. Since there is no more money left to buy these commodities for cash he has adopted another method of selling them in exchange for labor, and makes out checks for this amount. My Lord, in the month of July of last year, there came to this Garrison a party of Indians, who live on the coast near the Bahama Channel with a large quanitity of amber, some of which they presented to the Governor, the rest they gave in exchange for goods, and because a few of the soldiers bought some in exchange for clothing he was exceedingly angry. When these Indians left the land he had them followed by two rowboats with soldiers. He finally sent Don Alonzo Menendez with goods that he should bring him all the amber he could obtain, he also sent out others. The Lieutenants were Don Alonzo Menendez and Juan Dominguez and Alonzo Garcia. This trading for amber was carried on for six months. They used up all the iron implements. At first we thought that these implements were broken and thrust aside as worthless, soon, however, we discovered they were used to trade for amber, as well as five hundred tons more of iron which was brought from New Spain. All this was paid for from your Treasury. The amber was sold in Havana for the sum of forty thousand dollars. In the meantime the Fort has been allowed to suffer, it is falling to pieces in many places, the timber that was cut in the forest has rotted and the troops' time and iron implements are all used in the trade for amber. The infantry and other persons drawing a salary from your Highness have been on several occasions in a great rage with the Treasurer who abuses them and threatens them that Don Diego Rovellado will have them killed in the field—the guards, for the slightest offense, are beaten through the streets, and even imprisoned in the Church of San Francisco, and at times when he can catch them in his own house he slaps and beats them unmercifully. In a year and a half that he has been Governor he has only once complied with the laws of the Church, confessing and receiving the communion publicly. He says that every one can do as he pleases; that he does as he pleases. At the Fort he does not have the flag hoisted, only two guards at night and their round is an easy one, but he takes the men to guard his house every night, paying them a few dimes, and in the day he takes others to whom he pays two or three dimes, notwithstanding that your Majesty sends money each year to pay these men, but I am told that Don Diego Rovellado has paid the judge some five or six thousand dollars and he can escape free from any charge made against him. All that I state to your Highness in this letter, you may be quite sure is the truth, and I hope you will deem it proper to relieve your vassals from this unnecessary suffering. May God guard you and make you happy for many years. No SIGNATURE.

St. Augustine, Fla., November 20th, 1655.

The Unwritten History of

His Lordship: A. D. 1657.

Having begun the conversion of the Indians in the Province of Apalache at the close of the administration of Governor Louis Harristenir, who was immediately succeeded by Dannian de las Vegas. He placed a few soldiers in this Province to guard the going out and incoming of vessels. Having been imformed that they entered and left the Port, and there was no one to give any report of them. This guard was kept there during the assumption of power by Benito Ruiz Salazar and the Auditor Nicolas Ponce de Leon, until the Sergeant-Major Don Pedro Harristenir entered as Governor. This latter, to please the Friar, he not only dismantled the estates of your Majesty in those parts, but he also retired the Lieutenant and soldiers who assisted him, having no one to administer justice to the Natives, nor to give information concerning the Post, and so, immediately upon my taking the place of Governor, having been informed by the General Governors and other notables who were convened in Havana, and notified further by all the principal people of this Garrison who demonstrated how necessary it was to have a Lieutenant in said Province to guard and advise, as there had entered a vessel of the enemy, and the natives had aided them and supplied them in exchange for furs, hatchets, knives and other goods, without its being known in this Garrison. For this reason I named to the position Captain Antonio Sartucha and two soldiers with the instructions which I send enclosed—so that justice might be administered to the Natives, it being too laborious and the distance too great for them to come to this Garrison to adjust their quarrels and differences and to guard the Port and advise me. In a few days after his arrival he notified me of another vessel of the enemy (pirates) who had entered the Port. He asked for aid for infantrymen, which I sent him, to the number of forty, in command of Captain Gregorio Bravo. Before this aid reached him, the enemy was able to procure what they wanted. By pushing into service the natives, he was however able to prevent them from landing. It being urgent that I should go in person to pacify and punish the natives of the Province of Timagua, testimony of which decrees were made. I remit them to your Majesty. I passed on to visit the other Provinces and investigate the condition of the harbors. I did this with the consent of all the Casiques, and the approved judgment of Fray Francisco de San Antonio and other Friars, with the advice also of the Treasurer of the Royal Hacienda, and many of the reformed natives. I left in command the Sergeant-Major Don Adrian de Canizares, being a person of experience and trustworthy, giving him twelve infantrymen with which to defend the Port and coast of these Ports, and that he should administer justice to the Natives for which purpose I elected a syndicate of Friars who work in said Province, and some of their friends. Having determined upon this at the time you ordered me to be vigilant and careful, since the English enemy had attempted to occupy one of the Ports of this Province, according to information given your Majesty by Don Diego Cardenas, ambassador to England, and had been sent to me by Field Marshal Don Juan Montiano, Governor who was of Havana—information he gained from some prisoners, which confirms the information you had. There has been a fleet of the enemy on these coasts of Florida and the Bahama Channel. Although I had intended to increase the force of soldiers, build a Fort and found a settlement of Spaniards as I reported was agreed upon in the visit, which testimony, and that of the taxes and good government I remit with the decrees. I have desisted from this on account of the many contradictions and opposition of some of the Friars, who with the pretext that the vicinity of the Spaniards would be dangerous to the conversion, and who do not consider that this danger has a remedy, and it would be much more dangerous that the enemy should occupy that Port and plant foot on your territory and fortify themselves in a province so rich and abundant as those of Apalachicola, the knowledge of which the enemy is sure to be fully aware, and the danger would be irreparable and would lose in totem the conversions of these Provinces, and this Garrison would be unable to dislodge the enemy, from the distance at which we are, and that we could not scatter our forces, being too few of them, besides the consequences and damage which would accrue from pirates on the coast of Havana and the Bahama Channel—and there is no way of reaching us under five or six days of sailing. Finally your Lordship, the greater part of these conversions are reduced to three Provinces where Friars officiate—they are the Provinces of Guale, Tunnuqua and Apalache. In the two first there are few Indians, because for some time they have been diminishing, many having died out from the plague and small-pox which has been raging. The same is the case in Apalache, and in a few years very few will be left, and even now the condition they are in, it is unnecessary to assign as many Friars as you have. Besides their conversion would long be delayed owing to the great distance from this Garrison, the impassable roads and untold difficulties in sending relief, even should your Majesty send the wherewith to do so. Food must be carried eighty leagues from this garrison to the Province of Apalache and Chacata, on the shoulders of men—the burden is often more than they can carry. Although I have been admonished to relieve the twelve soldiers and Lieutenant for the good of the natives and the benefit they receive. I have sent persons there to remedy the evil, and seeing all I have herein stated that you may order things as you deem most advantageous and I shall carry out your orders regardless of the petitions of the Friars, who only base their objections in not wanting the Spaniards about them, as in their present condition they are absolute masters of the Indians.

May God preserve your Catholic Majesty.

DIEGO ROBELLEDO.

St. Augustine, Fla., October 18th, 1657.

A. D. 1657.

Things are in a most disastrous condition in Florida, there will soon be no government left, if God does not help us. The Casique of Tarihila refused to send some of his principal Indians to St. Augustine with heavy loads of corn. I don't know why the Governor insisted on this labor, but the Casique gathering together the other Casiques insisted that their principal Indians should not be made to do this work that they had vassals to perform their labor. The Governor took the refusal much to heart, and as a man of so little experience insisted until he caused them to rise. They said they were not slaves; that to obey God they had become Christians—they had never been conquered, but had listened to the word of God the Priest had taught them. So the Casique of San Martin at the head and all the Casiques who would follow him, which were the Casiques of Santa Fe, Potano and San Pedro, who marched from San Francisco and San Mateo with the others, making in all eleven Casiques, entered and hung the Governor. Think, your Fatherly Majesty, of such happenings. In a land where such war is carried on, I cannot tell you of the atrocities perpetuated by these poor Florida Indians. Nor do you understand how the Island of Jamaica is settled by the English, who have it well fortified with three strong Forts, and all the harbors are guarded. All prisoners from there tell us, and all who come from there tell us that now, in this month of May forty store ships arrived for them, and it is their intention to take Cuba. This has been known here and in Havana by mail, which has come. It is very important to notify you of all this, for soon it will be impossible to travel from here to Spain nor from there here. By giving this information I feel that I fulfill my duty, and you can act towards your vassals in a fatherly manner. FRAY JUAN GOMEZ.

St. Augustine, Fla., April 4th, 1657.

CHAPTER IX.

A. D. 1662-1670.

Report of Alonzo Aranqui y Cortez concerning the auditing of the accounts and condition of the Royal Treasury—Reports the finding of a large hill supposed to be a silver mine—Report of Jaun Cebadilla to his Majesty—The Governor not to keep the keys of the Royal chest—The administration to be adopted with the negroes—Too much harshness shown the Royal employees—Francisco Guerray Vega reports a Captain of the Garrison for indecency and offense to his superiors, for which same he was reprimanded and imprisoned as a warning, then given his liberty—The King to the Captain-General of the Provinces of Florida—Instructions as to the continuance of the passage to Marcana Guale—Founding the town of Santiago near Augustine—The performing of certain duties by soldiers for which money shall be paid—Soldiers shall be permitted to raise crops which are their principal sustenance — That the Governor shall not employ the people of the town in personal work for personal aggrandisement—But shall look that he, the Governor, shall look to the needs and wants of the people—By order of the King, 1670.

To His Catholic Royal Majesty:

Having presented before the tribunal on behalf of the Royal officers of Guadalapara the sworn bills, and others not sworn to, by which were adjusted and proven the accounts of your administration which had been running from the 7th of March, 1663, up to August 15th of the same year, it was found to result in a liquidated balance in favor of your Royal Treasury. Information of which was immediately sent to Don Geronimo de la Luna, judge for your Majesty, that he should have it delivered to the Treasury. He provided an Auto ordering Don Diego Salazar, Treasurer, to place it in the Treasury. This person replied to him stating that he had no money whatsoever from Jacon or Virginia. The infantry I sent out to investigate tell me that in the Province of Apalache there is a very large hill, which, in their opinion, is a silver mine, from the specimens found in the ground and from pieces they picked up on the hill and brought as samples. Persons who are versed in such matters say that from their accounts they must be mines.

As these matters do not admit of delay, and much care and caution is required, I am myself going to investigate the matter thoroughly, and give you a long and detailed account, being absolutely necessary for the tranquility of this Province. May God preserve your Majesty for many years.

ALONZO ARANQUI Y CORTEZ.

St. Augustine, Fla., September 8th, 1662.

To His Catholic Royal Majesty: A. D. 1666.

On the 27th of November of this year we received a document from Your Royal Highness with six orders containing the form and manner in which the

Old St. Augustine

Royal Treasury must be conducted in its administration and other things which were herein referred to, and what has passed in the accomplishment of them. The order in which your Majesty states that the Governor is not to keep the keys to the Royal Chest, but that your officer alone must keep them, and that an account must be kept and sent to this Treasury each year. We notified him and he obeyed, but as to its accomplishment he desired us to say nothing to him about it, as things were different here from other places—because all allowances and pay are collected by his order, and thus he wishes the keys to the chest where the money is kept. As to the accounts, he will provide them as should be just, which is the same answer he gave before as shown in the accompanying letter. The order for the administration that must be adopted with the negroes was obeyed by the Governor, and all are placed in compliance with it. We also notified him of the order your Majesty sent, reproving him for speaking so harshly to your Majesty's Royal Employees.

As the order sent by your Majesty regarding the labor of the estates, all necessary steps have been taken. The one received stating that hereafter one of your employees should be present at the paying of the workmen, and the providing of supplies and ammunition for these forts, was obeyed, and although the Governor also obeyed in the fulfilment of it, he did not do so to the letter and there has been trouble between us ever since. JUAN CEBADILLA.

Your Highness:

Don Francisco Larra whom your Majesty has had the mercy to send as Captain of a Company of soldiers to this Garrison of St. Augustine, Fla., is a person of such daring, restless and bold and has a mind—who is led astray by the impulses of his will—that with his manner of acting and talking he has given offense to the better and greater part of the people of this Garrison, not excepting the Ecclesiastics whom he offends and speaks in such abusive and indecent a manner of their character. And so on this account as well as the little respect with which he treats me, not paying the slightest attention to my office extrajudicially. I have admonished him in the kindest terms to correct his ways and fulfill his duties as Captain of the Infantry—not alone was this effort a vain one, but he took a bold and daring step with me, in the presence of the Ministers and principal people of the Garrison—for this incivility and profanation I had him imprisoned in the Fort, expressing to him my wrath and indignation, a copy of which I send you. With this as a warning, I then had him set at liberty. I beg your Highness that seeing this, you will proceed as you think best for the peace of this Garrison. May God give you the prosperity of a Christian.

FRANCISCO GUERRA Y VEGA.

St. Augustine, Fla., September 2d, 1666.

THE KING.

To My Captain-General of the Provinces of Florida:

The principal people of the town of Santiago de Tolomato have written me a letter on the 21st of

March, 1658, that Don Luis Reyes y Borhas, being Governor of those Provinces, laid the foundation of the town of Santiago, which is three leagues distant from the Garrison of St. Augustine with the intention of continuing a passage to Morcana Guale and surrounding Provinces and although at the founding there were many, only about thirty remained including Casiques and persons of standing, to continue the work. They beg that you will send more people, since they are quick and disposed to work, so that they may complete the passage as far as San Juan, a distance of twelve leagues, as much for the relief of the soldiers as other things that may occur. That they should not be called upon to perform other duties, as they have been by the Governors who has not recompensed them for their services. Calling upon them to unload vessels arriving at the Garrison, cut timber from the forests and other services not in their line of duty, taking them from their labor when planting corn, which is the principal sustenance for themselves and families, causing them to lose their crops and suffer hunger. Having seen in my Council of the Indias what I said to my Judge, it has seemed right that I should order and command you, as I have done, that hereafter you do not employ the people of said town in your own personal work and that you proceed to preserve them and relieve their wants by every possible means in your power and you will serve me best.

I THE KING.

Madrid, February 26th, 1670.
By order of the King our Lord.

JUAN TUBIZA,
Chairman of the Council.

CHAPTER X.

A. D. 1671-1673.

'Tis the judgment of the Court that Pedro Menendez received the title of Governor of Florida by right of conquest, Captain-General and Commander of the Fleet by appointment of the King, Don Felipe, the Second, as well as other positions of trust because of his valor and faithful service and that these titles shall be given to his legitimate heirs and for which same the Don Gabriel Menendez Tarres y Aviles doth petition and it is the judgment of this Court that said titles shall be so conferred—Important papers burned in Simancas—Manuel De Mendoza gives information commanded by his Majesty as to the designs of the English enemy—The discovery of the South Sea by the four vessels sailing through the Straights of Magellan—Condition of this Garrison and fortification and other Provinces implores assistance for completing the work already begun—Report of Francisco De La Guerra y Vega to the King concerning an Englishman taken prisoner while he was Governor—The prisoner was one of a crew who landed in the Province of Guale—The Indians killed seven men, imprisoned three and two women—They proved to be part of company coming over to settle in St. Elena—This man, who was second in authority in **the settlement, I detained as a prisoner, putting** *him on soldier's rations—He was turned over to*

my successor upon the expiration of my term of office—An effort was made to break up this settlement upon your Majesty's soil, without success, however. (1673.)

JUDGMENT OF THE COURT.

The Governor, Don Gabriel Menendez Torres y Aviles, sets forth in the preceding petition that His Highness the King Don Felipe II (whom God grant may come to glory) agrees with the Governor Pedro Menendez y Aviles, Knight of the Order of Santiago, that his uncle, brother of his grandfather, had agreed about the year 1565, that he, the said Pedro Menendez, had to discover all the provinces of Florida, settle and build in them two or three towns, all at his own expense, for which service your Grace granted him the title of Governor of said Province and lands of Florida, with all the privileges and prerogatives that are granted the other Governors of Castile—and that having set sail to accomplish this, and make these settlements with a private galleon of his own, of 900 tons, and many other ships and vessels which he also carried at his own expense and having conquered, as he effectively did. the said Province, and having settled and established two towns in it, which are today flourishing and supplying this crown, even before completion of this conquest. Your Majesty has named him Captain-General of the Royal Fleet which is to be commanded and joined in Santander against the English, commanding him to assist in this military exploit, notwithstanding that he is under obligations, in the first place, by the treaty and agreement he had made of discovering all the land of the Province of

Florida within the given term of three years counting from the day he embarked and set sail in the Bay of the Port of Cadiz with the fleet he carried for said conquest. Being of the greatest importance the business for which the Royal Fleet was formed and arranged, and while he was preparing and getting it ready, the said Governor Menendez de Aviles died— and by his death the Duke of Medina Sidonia was immediately named Captain-General. Afterwards having been asked on the part of the legitimate heirs of the said Governor Pedro Menendez de Aviles, the accomplishment of all these services which your grant had offered him, it was contradicted by the Attorney-General of this Court—taking advantage of one of said agreements which reads: "That if in the expressed term of three years the Governor Pedro Menendez de Aviles should not have finished and completed in all the said conquest according to agreement, neither your Majesty nor any other Kings, your successors, should be bound to fulfil any of the rewards offered." For this reason the heirs brought suit against the Attorney-General which was continued. For sentence, by revision of the Court it was ordered to be given to Don Martin Menendez, oldest brother of the petitioner, the title of perpetual Governor of said Provinces, as had been done with his uncle, and besides they were to give him forty thousand ducats of silver.

Withholding the charge of the Indias to augment from the right of succession which his uncle left established, and a fishery in said Province which the said Don Martin should select without any remuneration for the many expenses he incurred in the conquest, Don Martin Menendez having died without issue, or

Old St. Augustine

heir to his estate, the petitioner asked they expedite the title of Governor upon him, as it was expedient. Although endeavors have been made in the archives of Simancas to find these papers, they have not been found, and it is said they were burned in the fire which occurred in these archives. Imploring your Majesty's order that the pre-eminence and prerogative be reserved and observed as with the title of all the other courts and marquises of Castile, and also in consideration of the services rendered by the Governor his uncle, and other Generals of the Indias who were members of his house. Having seen in the Council of the Indias the petition and letters patent of nobility, and considering the great services done by Pedro Menendez de Aviles in the conquest of Florida as well as in other positions of trust where he has acted with so much valor as to deserve that his King Felipe the Second should have voluntarily given him the title of Governor, and that his successors continue to occupy positions as Generals—his house having spread such glory and honor as to be noted, it has seemed well that your Majesty should grant the petitioner the title of Castile, that he may enjoy the honors he so well deserves as a reward for his many and remarkable services. Your Grace will command that which is most deserved.

Madrid, November 28th, 1671.

Sire:

By Cedula of January 20th of this year, your Majesty commands me to give information regarding the designs of the English enemy. Also of the discovery of the South Sea by the four vessels which sailed through the Strait of Magellan, from which I had news that they arrived at Baldivia dismantled. A German Captain was in command. He showed great zeal in serving you. He gave a long account of the Viceroy of Peru, and what he intended doing. The Government Places under my charge are the Garrison of St. Augustine, Harbour and Port of Apalache and the river St. Catherine, a frontier of St. Elena, where the English enemy are at present; a few other less important harbours, all of which I desire to have guarded as by your orders I am obligated.

As regards this Garrison, head of this Province, and the state of the Fortification which is being built and the designs of the English enemy and the overtures made by them. This being a frontier of the Province of Guale where I have stationed some infantry to watch the movements and intuitions of the enemy, and where they could detain them, while I sent aid and as strong a reinforcement as possible. It seems the proper thing for us to have sufficient troops there to impede the approach of the enemy on this Garrison and place sentinels all along to notify should they approach by land or sea. As to the Province of Apalache which falls almost in the bosom of Mexico. I am sure it is a place of no less importance than this Garrison, rather I should say more so, being thickly settled and reached by land from all the Provinces far as New Mexico, and all others still to be discovered far as the Strait of David, of which the German Captain discourses at such length in his statement. Besides, it is a fertile land, and much longed for by the enemy as it is noted for its agriculture, for which cause it should be well settled and fortified, its Harbour should have a good fort and at least one hundred infantry who could at any rate give the English enemy some trouble to occupy it or set foot in said Province. This should be done to prevent any damage, not alone in the Province, but to vessels plying the Mexican path. I implore you to look into the matter with the care and attention the case requires. So far as I am concerned, I have made every effort in my power to secure and protect it. I shall try to push this building through rapidly, that I may go and reconnoitre that Province, carrying with me the military engineer, Ygnacio Daza, who resides in this Garrison, that he may point out what is needed at present. I implore your Majesty most earnestly to look with pious pity upon your Royal Provinces and send all the assistance you can to complete this building and the other works of which this Garrison stands in such need, lacking all the means of protection by which we can serve your gracious Majesty.

May God spare you for many years.

MANUEL DE MENDOZA.

St. Augustine, Fla., Dec. 15th, 1672.

Your Majesty: 1673.

In a letter of Yours of the present month and year, you tell me that seeing in the Council a letter which was received, written in English, it was agreed that I should inform you of what had happened to an Englishman, said to be prisoner in St. Augustine, Fla., where I was Governor. The cause and pretext for making him a prisoner. Complying with what your Majesty asks, I inform you in the following manner:

About the end of May of last year there arrived in one of the ports of the Province of Guale, which belongs to the Christian Indians, an English vessel. Some of the crew having landed in a launch, the Indians of that Province killed seven men, imprisoned three men and two women, then the vessel with all speed turned and went off, not giving time that from St. Augustine, where I was Governor, we should send help to those Ports to aid in imprisoning them. Bringing me these prisoners I ordered that their declaration be taken, at which I was present. They declared that they had come over with vessels to settle in the Port of St. Elena, distant from the Garrison of St. Augustine forty or fifty leagues north. In the month of June of last year there came to the Garrison a soldier with the news that the vessels had returned and entered the same Port, reinforced and with the flag of truce, the captain and four other men had landed and that speaking to a Lieutenant in command of the infantry on guard, they told him how they were establishing a settlement near St. Elena, with two hundred men, and that they came in search of the prisoner, delivering at the same time to the Lieutenant two letters from the Governor of that settlement, written in Latin, in which he asks that the prisoner be delivered, if not. they declared themselves enemies.

With this news I called a general meeting of the Royal Officers and Commanders of the war, from which resulted that all agreed it was the better way to serve God and your Majesty, and secure the quietude of those Provinces, to break up said settlement, and that

Old St. Augustine 119

we should go to work before they fortified themselves and take possession of more land. For this purpose they prepared themselves and equipped three vessels at that time in Port. The Chief in command being appointed by the Board, assigning him a number of warriors to obtain the object for which they went. A storm overtook the vessels and they could not get there in time and so arrived without accomplishing anything. Of the referred to notice, on two or three occasions, it was presented to your Majesty and to the Marquez of Macera, Viceroy of New Spain, always stating what was best to the service of God and your Majesty. To make every effort to dislodge the said settlement, it belonging to the Christian Indians, and they being new to our doctrine, might be easily influenced by the heresies of the English. And although not new to our Holy Faith, we might have the same doubts as they are a variable and roving people. It was advisable for your Majesty's service that we should dislodge them at that time, that they might not possess themselves of that Province and the interior land, and make themselves owners. It would not be well to have a settlement of a strange Nation on your Majesty's territory without your orders. From this information I awaited a reply to follow out the Orders from your Majesty and the Viceroy, and that together you would aid me, and with some help, as that Post lacks people, I detained the prisoner, not ill-treating him, in the house of one of his countrymen, allowing him military rations, which is what the soldiers in service have. As I was advised that the prisoner was the second person in authority in that settlement, I placed him under better security, that he might not escape and inform them of the lack of forces in the Garrison, for without doubt knowing it the settlement would come and take possession at very little cost. Just at this time my term of Governor came to an end, without having determined upon a method to work in this affair, I turned all over to the Governor, my predecessor, that he might act as ordered in the reply to my information. This is all that I can tell you regarding the English prisoner. By this the Council will know that I always worked with Christian zeal, trying to stop anything opposed to the increase of our Holy Catholic faith. God preserve you many years.

FRANCISCO DE LA GUERRA Y VEGA.
Madrid, July 12th, 1673.

CHAPTER XI.

A. D. 1675.

Letters to the King from the Governor, Pablo Ita Salazer—The oath administered in the tower of the old Fort, which is tumbling down—The Garrison in want of supplies and ammunition—No warehouses—Exposed to the fatalities of the weather—The Fort in danger from pirates—Necessary to use Spanish daggers for the land side protection—More money badly needed to finish the works—Importance of the Castle to the Garrison—A pentagonal form recommended — A hundred men needed to guard the Castle—The Viceroy of Spain did not send the ten thousand dollars—Fort in danger from pirates—Two hundred leagues from Havana and five hundred from New Spain.

Sire: A. D. 1675.

I have repeatedly given you an account of the manner in which I assumed control of this Government, taking the oath of fidelity in the tower of the Old Castle, which is almost in ruins, the artillery dismounted and scattered as if on a beaten field of battle. The blind obedience my duty demands in any employment of your Majesty, forces me to again repeat the condition of things. The old wooden Fort is in ruins, the stone one incomplete and with no defense whatever. No income or means to finish it. In the commissary department only one hundred "arrobas" of corn, and no other produce of any description. The Garrison is in the greatest want, as no vessels with supplies have yet arrived from New Spain. Seeing that we could not hold out three weeks longer, I seized two small vessels carrying about two thousand arrobas of corn. As the Fort was in such a demolished condition, with no defense and exposed to losing what was done, I detained these vessels, intending to give them some amount of embargo, conceding to each his share, but having communicated it to the Royal Officers, they thought it too severe treatment and that I should pay freight and the conquered's pay; that it would be better to pursue such a course. I let the matter stand for the present, retained the crew and the vessels I sent to bring peons to continue the building of the Castle, which is so absolutely important. This was done with the greatest care and promptness, as demonstrated on the maps I submit to you. Being entirely without means for carrying on this work, I implore you will send it. The Fort has neither walls nor moat, some of the ramparts only half finished, no means of closing it to make it secure. It would seem that they have been careless in the guarding of the Fort, sending only twenty-five men each day to do duty when it should have at least one hundred men constantly on the watch. I repaired things as well as I could for the lodging of the men and guards that they might stay in, as is done in Flanders and Milan and other places, but the Officers refuse to occupy them, stating they are in no condition nor have they sufficient conveniences for them to go in. As it will be profitable and advantageous to you, I implore you again not only to send the money but the order compelling them to enter at least

one hundred to guard the Castle. May God guide thee
in what is right. PABLO ITA SALAZAR.
St. Augustine, Fla., Aug. 23rd, 1675.

Your Highness:

Not to fail in my duty, knowing as I do from twenty-two years' service in your Majesty's States of Flanders and other ports, the importance of fulfilling. It has seemed necessary for me to give you a full and detailed account of the fortification being built in this Garrison by your Royal Order. I have already informed you of the condition I found it in, on assuming control of this Government of Florida. Considering it one of your defenses and territory under whose banner it was conquered, I have taken the greatest pains to investigate matters thoroughly. At first I could not give as true a statement as I should have wished, seeing so many faults and errors; but the untiring efforts I have made to ascertain facts have brought to light certificates of the enormous cost of this building. Being a place for the defense of the Bar, or entrance to the Harbor, I find that by making this fortification in a pentagonal form the bulwarks will point directly towards the Bar serving to defend from and towards an attack, and by building a battery it covers us in a measure from the enemy. Wishing to discuss this matter I called a meeting of the Royal Officers showing them the great saving of cost to the Royal Exchequer; but they seem opposed to the plan and, having no orders from your Highness, I am obliged to leave the work as it is. My greatest desire is to finish it and have the opportunity of defending

124   *The Unwritten History of*

Remains of the St. Augustine City Gateway.

it with my life. As on other occasions in other places, I have exposed that life. God grant you a long life.

PABLO ITA Y SALAZAR.

St. Augustine, Fla., Nov. 23rd, 1675.

Sire:

Having done me the honor to appoint me Mayor of the new city of Vera Cruz and port of San Juan de Ulloa, you still further honored me by appointing me Governor of Florida.

I immediately began an investigation of the state of the Old Castle and the new stone one being made by your order. In the first place I found it had the shape which will be clear to you in the report and letter of the same date as this. Secondly, they continued with many difficulties the building of the new one, as the Viceroy of New Spain has not assisted with the ten thousand dollars a year to which this Garrison is entitled by provision of your Majesty, and as you have no money or other effects in your Royal Chests to supply the wants, I have made it known to the Archbishop and Viceroy of New Spain by report and petition, showing them how urgent it was to send us a certain sum for the continuance of the building. I also notified the Judge of the Royal Audience of Mexico, as is evident through all that I place before you also what I have forwarded to the general finance office, who refused to send any sum whatever until I had from this Garrison given a report of the state of the building of the Castle, and the distribution made of the salary assigned since I took possession of this Government. I found the Port in a most dilapidated condition with no defense. I took the oath of fidelity as you ordered, and not to be wanting in my duty as a faithful vassal, as by being this, I have merited the great honors you have bestowed upon me in the field. Having taken the oath I received different Royal Cedules, among them one in which you command the Viceroy to send ten thousand dollars more for the building, and that the citizens and soldiers aid as far as they are able, as is done in other places, as the benefits redound to their good and security. I must tell you that they do, coming in person to assist in the building, with the accustomed punctuality which is all they can do, because this Garrison is composed of a few married soldiers who are extremely poor, their income not exceeding the salaries earned each year. This being a land of no commerce nor communication by entrances or departures of vessels, there being no produce or other necessaries with which to accummulate an income. And although you pay their salaries they never receive it in full, as they must first assist in the buying of accoutrements for the three vessels that bring the supplies. From their salaries they have also paid for the repairs of the Old Castle and the furtherance of the new building, warehouses, Royal Houses and all other necessary things which present themselves in a post, as you have not assigned to this Garrison any means for similar expenses, nor is there anything in the Royal Chests. There are no rents of any kind to supply them and it is in charge only of Royal Officers. The poor allowance divided among the infantry and the state of the Castle will be evident to you from the reports sent you, and I assure you that having served you for a period of forty-two years in the armies of Germany, Flanders and Badajos, in none of them have I been so well pleased as in this one, for the many difficulties and dangers. The lack of means for completing the fortification, the invasions and the lack of forces in which I find myself, as you will see by the lists I forward you of the subjects who are disabled and old and enjoy the privileges of false muster through your kindness. The soldiers and sailors, who at present run on these vessels and are absent most of the time, and those who are on guard as sentinels. So, when the boats are obliged to go out for supplies I am left with about eighty men who can serve. Besides this, we have no ammunition nor supplies, so much so that when I arrived the want was so great that families were obliged to go in the woods and hunt for roots to keep themselves from starvation. So exposed and in need were they that had a vessel landed and offered them food they would have miserably surrendered. And we are always thus exposed to this fatality, because we have no warehouses of food supplies as in every other port such as San Juan de Ulloa, Acapulco and Morro of Havana, in these parts. My experience in Flanders, Castillo de Amberes, Gante y Cambria, they have supply stores of vegetables, biscuit, cheese and hung beef, enough to last at least one year. I have sent them supplies for a long time, for in cases of accident, and here on account of the distance and slowness of communication there should be more care. Havana, the nearest point, is two hundred leagues, and New Spain is five hundred, so you see the vessels have to sail a long way exposed to the fatalities of storm, weather and pirates. which can at any time overtake them. I have thought proper to place all these statements before you, as being so important to your Royal Service you may consider them. And I beg you will aid in this building of the Fort, by sending the required means for its continuance. It would be a very great affliction for these Provinces to leave it in its present state. While I have seen many castles of importance and great renown, none surpass this one, nor have been built at so small a cost in the Indies, as will be demonstrated to you in the accompanying certificates given by the Royal Officer. It seems that the peons earn only one real a day and three pounds of corn, making the twenty-five pounds come to eight reals, which is the correct price. Their living in other places would be at least four reals. Two of the Captains who assist in the building and hewing of stone, earn only six reals a day, where in other places they would make at least three and four dollars per day. All the material and other things needed are in other places placed convenient for the workmen, so that had it been built elsewhere than in this Garrison it would have cost more than eighty thousand dollars. I find it very damaging for this Garrison to be without any fortification. We are obliged to tear down the old Castle just next to it, and the new one is not yet closed in, so that we fear the enemy who with a much larger force could easily capture us. They are only distant fifty leagues, two days' sailing, and once that they were owners of this Port, they would be of the entire Province destroying all the conversions of the Indians who to the service of God are supported and protected by the King and a great trouble to your vassals who sail back and forth in the commerce with

Old St. Augustine

this America. Being owners, they would have all the ports, and with their pirates stationed everywhere that vessels should pass. I feel the Port a little more secure than when I came, for one of the bastions is about completed, and by closing the other side looking landward with a palisade of Spanish daggers and tuna, I can retire if it should become necessary. In the meantime your Majesty will kindly apply the means sufficient to finish the work as speedily as possible, as the petition states the danger and risk this Garrison is in. May God spare you many years of the work of Christianity.

PABLO ITA Y SALAZAR.

St. Augustine, Fla., June 15th, 1675.

CHAPTER XII.

A. D. 1675.

An effort to be made to dislodge the English from Santa Elena—Orders to complete the Castle—Appalache considered the best Province for settlement—Families from Yucatan for settlers, also the Carrabies—Supplies sent from New Spain—Barracks to be made in the Fort for the soldiers—Money sent to finish the new Castle, also supplies for the soldiers—The neighbors to assist in building the new Castle—Repairs on the bulwarks at Guale—Increase of troops ordered for St. Augustine—A Fortress ordered built at Appalache for the defense of that Province.

By dispatch of the same month and year notice was given Governor Pablo Ita Salazar of the commands issued to his predecessor and to the Viceroy of New Spain regarding the dislodging of the English from the Port of St. Elena, of which they had taken possession with the intention of settling near the mouth, which in effect they did, ocupying a passage called St. George. For this reason notice was sent the Sergeant-Major Nicolas Ponce de Leon to proceed to dislodge the English from this settlement, gathering all the forces of that Province and asking aid of the Viceroy of New Spain who was ordered to reinforce him with what he needed. He did not think there would be any considerable difficulty in accomplishing this, as

Old St. Augustine 131

from four English fugitives he had learned all they had done.

By another dispatch the Governor of Florida was told that the Viceroy of New Spain had notified them of having aided that Garrison with all the supplies needed. As to the hundred families he asked for, that should go as laborers for the increase and culture of crops, they would look into the matter and attend to his representation of it when the case came up, and he was specially charged to be very careful and watchful in completing the Castle and defense of that Garrison.

By Cedula of 1673 the Governor of Yucatan was asked to send to Florida twenty-four families of Indians—master weavers—for the increase of those Provinces for which purpose he would place himself in correspondence with the Governor of the Islands, that both might work out the best means of accomplishing it.

The Governor of Florida replied that the best and most desirable Provinces for the Spanish nation to settle would be Appalache and others very near it. It was exceedingly fertile, and if the settlers were laborers the crops would be very abundant. They gather wheat as abundantly as corn which is the general sustenance. It would be easy to grow the fruits, the land being level and easy to reach on account of the many navigable rivers—to cultivate the lands in cotton, grain and indigo, which grows wild in those Provinces and the crops lost for the want of some one to cultivate them—and it would pay beautifully. This could be increased by putting the twenty-four Yucatan families in for a limited time. Having seen all this in the Council, they again commanded the Governor of

Yucatan to place himself in communication with the Governor of Florida and try to send these families, since such great gain would result from it, to those who go as native Indians of Florida to whose Governor he ordered, if this was carried into effect to supply them with the necessaries as per order of Cedula of 1673.

By dispatch of this same year the Governor of the Canaries was ordered and informed of the statement made by the Government of Florida regarding the hundred families going over to settle, telling him the means which could be used, and that it be carried and quickly and effectively that they might have the chance of obtaining the settlements of these Provinces. The Council of War having seen what Governor Pablo Ita Salazar had to say of the lack of food from which the Province was suffering, and the lack of means for obtaining it, commanded the Viceroy of New Spain to send that Garrison the necessary supplies for six months in advance, both ammunition and food, on account of the condition of the Garrison, so that it could be prepared for any emergency which might arise, and not be without defense, and to give an account of its execution. It was also commanded the Viceroy to send the necessary money to Florida that they might make Barracks and lodgings in the Fort for the soldiers who entered as guards, that they might be comfortable under cover and suffer less hardships. He was advised that all should be done with as little expense as possible, and to communicate with the Governor to whom the same order had been given. He said Don Pablo Ita Salazar made a report of the state in which he found the building of the new Castle in

Florida, and the lack of means with which to continue it. The Council of War having seen this report notified the Viceroy to send the supplies of three hundred troops, the quota of that Garrison, and three thousand dollars to be expended in the delayed fortification of said Castle; approved by the Governor, it should continue the work of the Castle, and he was recommended to try and reduce the expenses to the absolute necessary. That the neighbors might help in the building, as they were interested, and it was for their own convenience and defense that they could assist without loss of time, and with the supply of three hundred troops who would remain in the Castle. That the number of soldiers there was so reduced it would not only pay the people well but there would be a surplus of capital to provide all that was needed. That this complement of infantry should be kept in the Garrison, and his Majesty had resolved to send a hundred more soldiers by the first opportunity. He again commanded the Viceroy to punctually supply the wants, so that no cause can stop the building of the Castle.

In a letter of August 24th, 1675, the Governor, Don Pablo Ita Salazar, reported to have decided upon making a roof or covering for the bulwarks at Guale, to put the powder and other ammunitions used in the Garrison, and a Barracks and guard house, because what they had was of wood and exposed to incendiaries. That the Royal Officers were so opposed he desisted in its execution to avoid unpleasant encounters until it should be known in the Council, and together with the reports of the Officers. He ordered the continuance of the Castle for better security and defense at the least cost to the Royal Treasury.

FORTIFICATION OF APPALACHE.

Don Manuel Cendiga, being Governor of Florida, reported among other things the need of infantry in that Garrison—of what they had, much was in the Province of Appalache which belongs to that jurisdiction. For this reason his Majesty resolved to increase the troops of the Garrison of St. Augustine. He commanded the forty-three missionaries and the Viceroy of New Spain to order the Royal Officers of Mexico to increase the supply of troops in Florida, so that the quota remain at three hundred and fifty, besides the missionary fathers who must punctually supply them each year and solicit their complement.

Don Pablo Ita Salazar, Governor of Florida, gave a report of the numerous infidel Indian settlements there were in the Province of Appalache, and that in the Province of Guale the English had a settlement at St. George. That with the vexations, killing and thefts, with the vicinity of one and the other the Christian Indians receive, we find the only remedy to be in erecting a fortification in the Province of Appalache and place in it one hundred soldiers, and a body of one hundred families around them. Then we might promise to keep them in obedience and subjection to this throne. The Council having seen this, ordered that at present they should prepare to make a fortress in the Port of Appalache in the best and easiest manner for the defense of that Port, and report by the first opportunity the time and amount required for building it. By still another dispatch he ordered the Governor to send a perfectly clear report of what he had already done regarding the fortress of the Port, and of all the Province; the spot best adapted for it, the form and disposition, forces needed for the defense, and if there would be any difficulty in opening up the entrance of the Bay, where it was built; the depth of the water, if vessels could enter, and of what tonnage; have a very careful and minute report from some one of experience and a master. Send a map and report attached of what this work will cost, giving your opinion so that seeing it and the information asked on the matter the most advantageous resolutions may be taken for the security and defense of that Province.

CHAPTER XIII.

A. D. 1680-1685.

Letter from Pablo Ita Salazer to his Majesty—Indians of the Province of Guale ally themselves with the English and together with over three hundred men make war against the Spaniards of the Island of St. Catherine—Surprising and killing the sentinels, only one of whom escaped to warn the Garrison— The people gather in the convent of a Friar and defend themselves from daylight until four o'clock, when aid from this Garrison reached them—The enemy retires — Natives of the Island greatly alarmed—Disquieting news of the intentions of the enemy upon this Garrison—Implores the aid of the King quickly that the English may be ejected from the land—Don Jaun Marquez Cabrera, Governor and Captain-General of Florida, gives an account to his Majesty of hostilities in the Provinces—Two Fleets, French and English, going and coming from Havana—Seize Fort Matanzas and after plundering, burn it to the ground—Is being rebuilt — Great depredations committed up and down the coast by the enemy—Indians and half-breeds taken and sold into slavery—Pushing the work on the Castle—Grieved over its slow progress, owing to lack of workmen—Begs to be allowed to retire because of age and long service— To Charles II, our principal Casique, the King— From the people of the territory of Habalache—

The King to the Governor and Captain-General of Florida concerning ten negroes from St. George who asked for the waters of baptism—A Sergeant-Major from St. George comes to claim them— Because they have become Christians the Spanish King decides to buy them—After receiving a receipt they are to be set at liberty, each one given a document to that effect—The King reprimands Don Diego Quirago for not immediately attending to these matters—Orders a full account to be sent as soon as it is accomplished.

Sire: A. D. 1680.

In a letter of April last year I stated to you the misgivings I felt about the English who have populated the Province of Carolina and River St. George. In November of the following year I repeated this with some evidence, and such a plan or a map from the River St. George to Mobile. Afterwards I was notified that five Englishmen had put to flight one of the Towns and penetrated as far as the Province of Guale, which belongs to the jurisdiction of this Garrison, where they came to take declarations and give information concerning the coming of the English to those parts; all of which I submit to your Majesty.

My duty today is to give an account of what happened in the Province of Guale this year. The Chuchumacos, Bechizes and Chulucas who were at war among themselves, but had maintained friendly relations and trading with this Province, became friendly with the English and have declared themselves our enemies. They made an invasion first on the Island of Guadalquiri in Guale, then on the main land they killed and scalped a number of the Natives until these latter rallied and, with one of our Lieutenants at the head, sallied forth and repulsed them. A few days later they made an entrance on the Island of St. Catherine, one of the frontiers, with a force of over three hundred men. They killed the Sentinels who were six in number, one only escaping, who gave the alarm and the citizens were able to defend themselves. There were forty-five Spaniards from this Garrison and about a hundred Natives. They took refuge in the Convent of the Friar, who teaches the Gospel in that Province, Captain Francisco Suentes, whom I sent two years ago to take charge of that place, who defended himself and army with great valor and distinction from daylight until four o'clock in the afternoon against these Indians, who were armed with firearms. Instantly upon receiving information of the danger I sent aid to the number of thirty soldiers on foot and a vessel with eighteen marines. When they arrived the enemy had retired. I am assured that among them were several Englishmen who instructed them in the use of the firearms, which consisted of long guns. This caused great consternation and horror among the natives who at first evacuated the Island of St. Catherine, but am informed have since returned doubling their forces. I had sent eight men to them from this Garrison and I am resolved to send twenty—it being a place of the utmost importance to this Garrison, as a protection against invasions and also to obtain food and supplies. The entrance to the Bar of Zapola is easy and distant from it, as you can see on the map, only two leagues. Information has been brought me by a pilot, who left here and was taken prisoner by the

French, that he overheard them say they would come to this Province, possess themselves of the Island and Bar of Zapala. This is damaging news, and my greatest trouble is lack of troops, for altogether I have only some two hundred and ninety. I have increased this with a few natives of seemingly good disposition, should a fight occur in this Fort, but so inexperienced that they could not support us. This Post is mainly composed of mariners, pilots, shipmasters and mates, twelve artillerymen, six widows and a few children to whom, through your mercy, you grant pay, and ten or twelve decrepit old men who by age are exempt from toil. I have twenty-four men in Apalache, distant eighty leagues, and two in Timuqua, two in the pass of Salamatoto, ten leagues distant from this Garrison. The sentinels of Matanzas and the Bar. All this causes me great distress as I should be obliged to repair to the field and I have no resources possible with so few people. Notwithstanding, I propose, with the help of God, to improve it, and thus will the conversions advance and secure the road to Mexico. It is expedient to run the English out of that land, and there are not two hundred firearms in the armory nor among the soldiers and natives. If the thirty lancers and hundred infantry I sent for three years ago had come, things would be in a different shape. With a hundred families to protect, a good deal of aid is needed as speedily as possible and your Majesty will send them promptly as to the interest of your service. God protect you.

PABLO ITA SALAZAR.

St. Augustine, Fla., May 14th, 1680.

Sire: A. D. 1682.

Don Juan Marquez Cabrera, your Governor and Captain-General of the Provinces of Florida, gives you an account of how since last February of this year they have experienced many hostilities in these Provinces from two French and English fleets who, since they discovered and settled with ten vessels they brought on these coasts towards the south, have taken and settled all the entrances and Ports, having seized seven vessels that were coming and going to the City of Havana, entered and plundered the Fort of Matanzas with no resistance from those within, and on another occasion in the same place, where there were forty-five Spaniards, captains, lieutenants and soldiers, there came four hundred Indians with firearms and arrows to one of the trenches at the edge of the two rivers at the foot of the Fort and this time they did not discharge a single shot, but set fire to the Fort and burned it, being of wood. I am again rebuilding it in the shape of a bonnet or cap with its inclinations bias, which it did not have before, with twenty-five stone houses, so that twelve or sixteen soldiers can defend it. On retiring they entered the River of Point Martin in Laungara, eighteen leagues inland and forty from this Garrison; thirty-five Frenchmen entered and plundered the estate Lachua, imprisoning the owner and some of his slaves and other persons and their servants. They were assisted in this by three of the neighbor Casiques, with sixteen Indians. As they retired they were met by an ambush who liberated the owners of the estate with the loss of one Indian. Although there were five Spaniards, with the degree of

Captain who enjoy the rank and pay, excused themselves on the occasion because they feared if they had any one to encourage them the enemy would not have left one. As soon as I received the news, although I am very scarce of people for the defense of the Castle, I made every effort possible to send the Sergeant-Major of this Post with forty soldiers as quickly as possible. Finding the enemy already embarked, I ordered him to obstruct the river, seeing the danger to this Province, not having had any orders from you to keep it open. Notwithstanding all the Sergeant-Major's efforts to place obstructions, I fear the enemy will invade this Garrison if only to see the Fort that is being built. It is to be in the shape I have shown you on the map, and plan I have given the Adjutant Alonzo Solano, superintendent of the work, a man of much intelligence and quite capable of carrying it on. At the time the French were destroying the estate Lachua the English landed at the bar of Mosquito Inlet; they killed ten Indians and captured eighteen. They had also captured the frigate that left this Post for New Spain; they captured it with a pirate vessel which had come from Jamaica, as testified to by the "Autos" I sent, in which I also stated the other hostilities and depredations as you can see in the Office of the Royal Council. It is a source of grief to me to see the manner in which they take these poor Indians and sell them into slavery, as they have done with many, selling them on the Island of Barbado. They even take the mixed ones, children of Spaniards and Indians. Although I am quite advanced on the building and defense of the Castle, I feel disconsolate when I think of the scarcity of troops and the inferior quality of those I have who are cowardly and pusillanimous as I have before represented them to you. I repeat it, in hopes that you will send me at least two good Captains and a hundred first class men. Besides being dastardly those I have, many of them are too old to be of service, having been retired and pensioned off. I am heartily sick of those who have been pensioned off, and of the children who have been pushed into service with no other object than to receive the pay. While mindful of the humane interests, this at times is exceedingly trying to my patience. And so, since the Fort is assuming such shape, I implore you to give the order needed of sending more men. I also implore your Majesty that having served you so many years without complaint against me, that you will replace me in this Garrison and give me permission to retire.

God grant you a long and prosperous life.

JUAN MARQUEZ CABRERA.

St. Augustine. Fla., July 16th, 1682.

CHARLES II, OUR PRINCIPAL CASIQUE, TO THE KING.

God, who with His power has created us from nothing, it being His will—we live, although with work and misfortune, it matters not how, so we live, with our limited understanding, every day without ceasing as we are commanded by our Creator, since He so wishes it, we praise and reverence Him. Leaving this apart we also, the nobility and all in general, old men and old women, children, orphans and disabled, as many as are found in this territory called Habalache, every day we say it seems to us, we do not reverence, embrace and receive in our hearts our principal Casique and King and his noble words. Saying this among ourselves it seems to make us more humble and disposed to receive your words when it reaches our ears. As at present, we could long since have written you, for the obedience we show you, and not waited for your many noble works, and to make known to you of what we are here seeing and suffering, being not only ourselves, but all in this world, who were created from nothing by the will of God. Our priests whose duty it is to care for our souls, cleanse them and absolve them, teaches us good things, and takes away and quenches in us ugly and evil things helping us on to be good Christians, as it is for this you have shown us such great mercy, and so we recognize it, and are believing with one heart. Second: Although we are ignorant people, we think that our hearts and souls belong to our Creator—our bodies and their government, and to whom they belong to teach and punish is to our Head, whom thou art, and whom we recognize as our chief Casique and King, and as the grass grows and has roots, bathed by the dews of night, so we and all your miserable vassals are nourished by your noble words, and although bodily we do not see you with our eyes, we take it from the one who represents you as your Governor and Captain-General— and to him we look as to you and as your words coming from him who we see, hear and understand, and guard, believing and obeying him—

Sire:

From information that I was able to gather by means of gifts to the native Indians, I succeeded in finding out the designs of the settlers of St. George and of the new settlement in St. Elena, where this Garrison was first — distant from here some sixty leagues. About 50 Indians, with orders from the Governor of St. Elena, were to enter the Province of Tamaqua, do all the damage and hostilities they could, taking prisoners and killing the natives. I immediately sent a dispatch by carrier to the Lieutenant of that Province to be on guard and care for the towns. It seems that some six hours before he received my notice, they had entered and destroyed the town of Afinca, a place of about sixty natives. About fifty men entered with sixteen guns and the balance with bows and arrows and machetes, everything exactly as I had been informed. They belong to the Yamares nation who have retired from this dominion and gone over to the English. They killed and carried off the prisoners as certified by a letter from the Lieutenant. I have restored as far as possible the Garrison of Tamaqua for the peace of its natives. If I had had the force sufficient I would have sent the vessels that I have to the settlement of Santa Elena and done them some damage, but, as it is, I have not sufficient forces for anything. The two Captains experienced in that part of the country are old, one of 70 and the other 60 years old. I am sorry to say, the enemy are settling in the interior, where they find the lands so rich and productive of all kinds of fruit. Should they come here they could easily capture us for the lack of men— we need men—more troops. I am informed that forty days ago, eleven vessels with seven hundred men, had been sent out from England. I am awaiting them with fear, for lack of men and ammunition we have. I also distrust my sentinels. I hope you will immediately send me reenforcements.

God preserve you, etc.

JUAN MARQUEZ CABRERA.

St. Augustine, April 15th, 1685.

THE KING.

To my Governor and Captain-General of the City of St. Augustine in the Province of Florida, and Field Marshal Don Diego de Quiraga y Lasada, in whose charge that Government is now:

The Royal officers of that City have given me an account in different letters of their having arrived at that Garrison ten remaining negroes, eight males and two females, from St. George. That they asked for the waters of baptism, it was given them, after which a Sergeant-Major from St. George came to claim them. Not appearing to be the proper thing to return them after becoming Christians, it was agreed upon with the Sergeant-Major to buy them with the money from my Royal exchequer for the sum of sixteen hundred dollars, granting a writing to that purpose, to pay said sum at a stated time specified. To satisfy this I sent to the new city of Vera Cruz for this sum of money which was brought and deposited in my Royal coffers of that city, advising the Governor of St. Augustine and notifying the Governor of St. George to send for it. It seems they came for it at the time the Governor was distributing aid to the soldiers. He had notified me of the receipt of this money, but not receiving a reply, he supposed I was not satisfied with the transaction, imploring I should tell him what to do with the negroes. The men had been put to work on the Fort, and the women the Governor had retained as servants in his household. He paid the cost of them, and he only awaited my orders. In view of all that he asks, through the judge of my Council of the Indias, it occurs to me to say to you that Don Diego Quiraga was wanting in his duty by not sending to pay the money deposited in the Royal coffers for the purchase of said negroes and in the word he had given the English. He should have considered that in refusing to deliver them to the English, it was done to protect the religion; this alone would have sufficed, being as I am such a Catholic. For any excess expended in their purchase, notwithstanding my failure in replying to him on this point, and so, it appears strange what this Governor has done. And so, that you perfectly understand what I order you, as I do order you, that of the first money which comes into my Royal coffers of that City you immediately pay up the whole amount, and give the Governor of St. George perfect satisfaction for the 1,600 dollars agreed upon for the sale. The defraying of this to be done as quickly as possible. And as a reward for having come to these provinces to live under the laws of the Gospel and become Catholics, I order that immediately upon receipt of this, you give them all their liberty in my name, giving each one, males and females, a document to that effect, so that seeing their example others may do likewise. As soon as you have accomplished this you are to send me a full account, as this is my will.

I, the King, sent by the King our Lord,
DON JUAN DE LA VEA,
Chairman of the Council.

CHAPTER XIV.

A. D. 1689-1698.

Letter of the Governor and Captain-General of Florida, Don Diego Quiroba y Losada, to his Majesty —Giving an account of a custom obtaining in the Garrison which he deems dangerous to its safety— That is, the ringing of the church bells at midnight, when the Host is taken out to administer communion to the dying until the same is returned, oftentimes lasting hours, which same drowns the fire of the sentinel across the river, who is to fire as many times as there are vessels sighted—This danger has been fully laid before the Priest, but to no purpose, notwithstanding the city has been in arms for some days awaiting the enemy—There is also testimony accompanying this letter of the same purport—His Majesty by a Cedule of July 18th, 1694, asks for a statement of the order pursued in the functions of the Edicts of Faith and Anathema and the places where they conduct the Holy Tribunal of the Inquisition—These questions answered by Severino Mausaneda, March 17th, 1690—In 1691 Governor and Captain-General of Florida, Don Diego Guiroga y Lorada, gives an account of a military review of St. Augustine—Of the great advantage and security to the city of building a sea wall extending from the Fort the entire length of the town, thus securing it against the sea which in storms comes up to the houses—

The soldiers and citizens subscribe ten thousand dollars and his Highness is implored to designate a sum to help to build this wall that the people will be convinced of his Highness' interest—The King, A. D. 1698, to the Governor and Captain-General, Don Diego Guiroga y Losada, of the City of St. Augustine, in which he rebukes the said Governor for unjustly taxing the Indians, whom he wishes civilized, and not treated alone as vassals, but as his children, attending to their comfort and want, and imposes a fine if the money sent to be spent for canvas and provisions be not paid to these Indians as per agreement—Extracts from the investigations of the Council, in regard to alleged excesses committed by the Governor of Florida, Don Francisco Moral Sanchez—Besides the scandalous reports certified to, is his ill treatment of a Captain of Grenadiers acting according to his own will instead of by military law—The Royal Officers protest—Certify to the truth of these investigations, and implore justice from the King—A report according to his Excellency's desire concerning affairs under Governor Don Francisco Marales Sanchez—The investigation shows that the facts set forth in the different papers and petitions sent to his Majesty to have been only too true—Impossible to put upon paper the strange, divers and extraordinary excesses committed by this Governor.

Sire: A. D. 1689.

Today I must give you an account of a custom I have found here, which might redound to the injury of this Garrison. It is that at any hour of the night when the Host is taken out to administer communion to the dying the church bells are rung and continue to ring until its return to the church, with the same solemnity as is done in the day time. Now, this might cause very serious results, as when we have the sentinel who is on duty across the river, to fire as many times as there are vessels in view, then the bells are rung and the people gather together. This makes us very attentive in listening for the firing and the noise of the bells at all hours prevents us from hearing and would give the enemy an opportunity of entering and capturing the Town. I always keep the Fort well guarded and am prepared, but as we know from so many occurrences in the Indias in the past few years, all the misfortunes of invasions have come from carelessness. I have solicited the Priest not to have this done and even refused to let him have the soldiers to follow in the procession, but he is very impertinent and says the church belongs to him and he shall do as it pleases him. Since the 28th of May we have been in arms awaiting the enemy, and I sent the Priest word not to ring by one of the soldiers, then by the Sergeant-Major—in spite of my message he rang the bells from half-past ten at night until half-past two o'clock. To avoid danger from this, I have given orders that none of the soldiers attend. If he desists from ringing I will allow him all the soldiers necessary. Things will work thus until your Majesty orders otherwise for the safety of this Garrison. God grant you long life. DIEGO QUIROBA.

St. Augustine, Fla., August 16th, 1689.

The Unwritten History of

TESTIMONY WHICH ACCOMPANIES THIS LETTER.

In the City of St. Augustine, Fla., May 28th, 1689.

The Captain of Cuirassiers, Don Diego Quiroba y Losada, Governor and Captain-General of this city and Province, by order of your Majesty.

Says: That this Garrison being in arms and awaiting signals since Sunday, the 22nd. The church has on several occasions rung the bells after midnight in taking out the Holy Sacrament, continuing the ringing for two hours or more, without ceasing. This is contrary to all customs in Spain and the Indias, where the sacrament is not carried in pomp after night, but only by the Priest, the sacristan and two other persons who carry the lights. In a close Garrison it is more strictly observed, and for that reason should be more strictly enforced in this Garrison, as such things are risky, especially as we are under arms, and injury might result, as it would give the enemy time and opportunity to accomplish their intentions. We are trying to stand on the defensive and it might injure this very church itself. For this reason I sent word to the Priest, Don Alonzo de Legurion. Parish Priest and Vicar of this city, in all due form by St. Sebastian Lopez begging him to cease the ringing and setting forth the danger which could result. That he should not go out in pomp, but ask for all the soldiers he wanted and they would be sent. He would not listen, and threatened the Lieutenant with excommunication should he return. Another message I sent by the Sergeant-Major, Pedro Arauda y Avellanedas, to whom he made the same reply, stating that the Church was his and he would ring when he pleased—it had been

Old St. Augustine 151

given him by the Pontificate, and the Governor had nothing to do with it, and must not meddle. Such language and conduct disturbs the public peace. That all this may be certified to I have ordered testimony taken of the case and had the Sergeant-Major and Adjutant Sebastian Lopez examined, and so I sent it and sign   DIEGO GUIROBA Y LOSADA.

Appeared before me, Alonzo Solano, Notary Public of the government, in the City of St. Augustine, Fla., as witness.   SEBASTIAN LOPEZ.

May 22nd, 1689.

Captain Diego Quiroba y Losada, Governor and Captain-General of said city, ordered to appear before me, the Adjutant, Sebastian Lopez, who is the actual Sergeant-Major in the Garrison, who was in my presence received and sworn in by the Notary Public, in the name of God and the Holy Cross, and having promised to tell nothing but the truth. Asked for the tenor of the Auto at the head of this Document, he said: That at about half-past two o'clock the bells of the church of this City were ringing. Having started out, his Lordship, the Governor, called him and ordered him to take a message to the Priest, telling him that he knew well that the City was in arms, the enemy being on this coast, and they had received signals that the vessels were in sight of the City, and to cease ringing the bells as the noise would prevent them from hearing the signal "to arms." That coming to the church he told the Priest to stop ringing, that it made too much noise. The Priest's reply was to order him to leave the church under pain of excommunication, the witness returned three times with the Governor's Message, but no attention was paid to his Lordship's Message, and the bells continued to ring. That this is the truth, under sworn oath he states and affirms and that he is twenty-two years old and he signs it.

SEBASTIAN LOPEZ TOLEDO.

Before me, Alonzo Solano, Notary Public and of the Government. It agrees with the original of which mention has been made and which I send. Executed in St. Augustine, Fla., on July 15th, 1689.

ALONZO SOLANO,
Notary Public and of the Government.

By Cedule of your Majesty dated in Madrid, July 18th, 1674, you ask for a statement of the order pursued in the functions of the Edicts of Faith and Anathena and the places where they conduct the Holy Tribunal of the Inquisition. And also the cause of the controversies offered by the city whenever they are performed and what has been done this year. The city to avoid all scandal resolved to allow the Commissioner of the Inquisition to conduct things his own way—taking testimony of all the proceedings to report to your Majesty. These acts have no fixed time, but left to the arbitration of the Commissioner who has them when he pleases. every two, three, and even six years. After discussion it was decided not to have them executed this year, as it is not a regular custom, and we wished to report before giving more examples of dissensions. For twenty years the City has allowed itself to be fined for neglect of duty in assisting at the performances. As there is no Tribunal of Inqui-

Old St. Augustine 153

sition here the Commissioner succeeded in getting the City to go to his house for him, and he, precedes the City. In church, his place to be on the Gospel side, with the humility recognized in such places. The decision of this controversy seems to depend on Law 20, Chapter 26, of the ninth recompilation of the Indias. This last, the Holy Tribunal of the Inquisition pretends is only understood by your Majesty, the Viceroys and Captain-Generals in whom are found a living representation. So that to represent the Holy Tribunal of the Inquisition the power is solely invested in your Commissioner—from this comes the act of tramping under foot your Government, whom the Commissioner tries to subdue in all, to his will, as well as the Notary Public and Ministers. That a stop may be put to his audaciousness it has seemed wise and prudent to make a report with testimonies attached to your Majesty, that you may act as you deem proper in the case.

May God grant you long life.

SEVERINO MAUSANEDA.

Havana, March 17th, 1690.

Your Highness: A. D. 1691.

Don Diego Quiroga y Lorada, Governor and Captain-General of the Province of Florida, in a letter dated January 8th, 1690, gives you an account of the general review which he passed on the soldiers of infantry and militia of that Garrison. He proposed the the advantages and security occurring to the City by building a wall from the Fort, the whole length of the City along the sea, seeing the danger in which it now is of being ruined by floods from the sea (which already comes up to the houses) when we have the slightest storm. The soldiers seeing the necessity of it, immediately offered what they could, the citizens of the Province doing likewise, that the work might advance. I send a certificate showing that the amount of the offering they have made is ten thousand dollars, and that they will use every effort to build the wall, and they have commenced to get out the stone and other necessary things. I implore your Highness to designate a sum to help build this wall, which is so important and that these poor soldiers and citizens may feel encouraged to give more, seeing that your Majesty helps them in such needed work, since nothing less depends upon this wall than the preventing a flood of the place and separating the Castle, losing all that has been spent in the building of it. The Board is obliged to represent you. What the voluntary contributions of the soldiers and citizens of the Province is for the building of this wall, estimate the cost of it, and how much will be needed to continue the work, and with this and what you order, the Count of Galva, Viceroy of the New Spain, must send to Florida the sum of two thousand dollars, that the Governor may apply it to this work, and that he inform the Board of the size, latitude and thickness, the design of it, that they may better understand it. And that the Royal Officers certify that said portion of the two thousand dollars was spent on this work, sending an exact account and cause. Then, the soldiers and citizens of Florida seeing that your Majesty takes an interest in them and helps them, will feel encouraged to continue subscribing. You will decide as most convenient.

Madrid, August 11th, 1691.

THE KING.

To the Field Marshal Don Diego Quiroga y Losada—My Governor and Captain-General of the City of St. Augustine, in the Province of Florida, or to the Person or Persons in Whose Care His Government May Be:

In a letter of June the 8th, 1640, it refers, among other things, that you have sought the means of spending the money assigned for the purchasing of canvas and provisions for the Indians of the Pass of the River Salamototo, as was evident by the certificate and agreement that together with the Royal Officers of that city you made. Seeing all in my Council of War of the Indians—how special attention was called to the new tax imposed for the canoes that serve as transports at the referred river, I have resolved to order and command you (as I do) that the moment you receive this order, that you revoke the one by which you have distinguished yourself together with the Royal Officers, as the agreement of the 1st of February, of 1698, being worthy of reproof, the one that you and they are working in this matter. without any orders whatsoever from me—as should always be the case in questions of this nature especially when my royal soul is so moved towards the Indians, my desire so great, that they should be civilized and treated not alone as my vassals. but as my own children subjugating them and attending to their wants and comfort. Thus you will proceed to revoke what you have done. Advise my Royal Officers by dispatch of the date that they take note of this resolution in the books under their charge—so that at all times it shall be evident. And I also command that you immediately have published and posted proclamations to this effect in all public places in the city and Province inserting to the letter in the proclamation the contents of this dispatch, and sending to the board by the first opportunity presenting itself, testimony of having executed this procedure. A fine of a thousand reals imposed upon you, to be remitted if you do not execute this order immediately in the form that I have imposed and commanded. And that the canoes remain and be paid as they have been up to the present, and as they were up to the date when you imposed the above expressed tax. And you shall advise me clearly and plainly what has been the amount of these taxes up to the date of receipt of this dispatch, and if there be any portion of it, you have it placed at once in my Royal Chest in that city, to remain there until receiving my further orders. So does it suit me and my Royal service.

THE COUNCIL.

Continuing the account of investigations which have been obtained and were promised in a letter of October 22nd to ascertain with certainty of the excesses committed by the Governor of Florida, Don Francisco Moral Sanchez.

The Council makes known that the events are so strange and extraordinary, which by divers means have been understood to have taken place in that Garrison and its administration, that the very excess itself stuns one with astonishment and paralyzes the credulity of our mind—but, having complied with his duty as commanded, he explains: That he is quite assured of the truth of the report of the Engineer Don Antonio Arredondo, who was an eye-witness and had no reason whatever to judge him otherwise than impartially, being in no conceivable manner dependent. That his report agrees in every particular with the other letters written of the excesses of the above mentioned Governor as will be recognized by the document which accompanies this and is certified to by the Engineer Arredondo at the continuation of them in a private declaration made by the decree expedited for this purpose.

That the few Indians of our faith represent and express their true sentiments, as indicated by a document I remit to this Council, through the Rev. Bishop of Micale, which they obliged Senor Arredondo to receive and remit to your Majesty. That other certificates of military and private individuals of that Garrison, with other documents which accompany this, and not only confirm, but add such scandalous excesses of the private life of that Governor, that it is impossible to find decent and decorous words with which to express them. And some of these words are from the mouth of religious Monks and Priests who affirm all these letters as well as the one written by Don Antonio Benavides—there are also later letters giving accounts of the same proceedings.

Besides the scandalous reports being certified to by all, in about the same manner, they accuse the Governor of his treatment of the Captain of Grenadiers Don Felipe de Iturrieta, commandant of the detached troops, forgetting his personal merits, and official position, and his being a person of implicit integrity. He had him thrust into prison in a most shameful and scandalous manner—even depriving him of the resources of writing—and after trampling him in every way he incriminates him for disobedience in the performance of his duties—a mere pretense, for it was that this Officer refused to neglect his duty or allow his men to do so, by being off guard at the Barracks, where it is imperative, according to all military laws that guards should be at their post. The Governor wishing the men for his private purposes ignored or formed false conception of military duties and suspended and imprisoned the Captain. Of the same nature is the charge made against him of violating the Royal ordinance and defying it—when he replied to the Governor in words which would rather indicate respect. It is a shameful act to treat an Officer of honor of his well known character, who has the heavy responsibilities which are recognized as belonging to said Captain, and are certified to in the statements of the circumstances, as also a petition in which is set forth all that has occurred, and imploring that justice be shown Captain Iturrieta that he may not be stigmatized. While all written in these reports and certificates are true, I did not depose him immediately from office until I received the report asked of the Bishop of Micale, knowing his prudence and virtue and that his word would be more approved than all else in the case. In the meantime while awaiting his report I am taking every step to conquer the difficulties which may arise to name a subject who can act in the interim, because it seems the need is so great that it is impossible to form any resolution whatever in the case pending in that Province, and this consideration has suspended all movement of removing him until the order comes for doing so. This in our judgment being more prudent, as the referred to Governor is so engrossed

Old St. Augustine 159

in his private affairs as certified to in the papers of Don A. Arredondo, in which he speaks of the Barracks for lodging the soldiers, and the looking into this matter belongs to the Viceroy of New Spain—that in proper time he take the precautions which he deems most essential.

Concluding with the disposal of the reports, and taking the less scandalous means to depose the Governor of Florida, Don Francisco Moral Sanchez, as he has not been forewarned of what is to happen, it seems doubtful which is the best means to adopt, we will therefore consider the matter with more deliberation proceeding in the safest and most certain way and rendering a personal account as quickly as possible thereafter. THE COUNCIL.

Excellent Lord:

In conformity with what your Excellency desires, and satisfying the private order sent me, asking a report and true statement of affairs under the Governor Don Francisco Morales Sanchez. To assure myself from a responsibility devoid of all partiality, and to the truth of the excesses perpetrated by this Governor and a few other private individuals and priests, of which that Garrison wrote you a complaint, asking that you immediatly depose the Governor and name some one in his place, *pro tem.,* so that your Majesty being informed, may place some one who looks more to your interests. For this purpose you sent me a blank dispatch, that in time, I might fill out with the names of the subject elected and the investigation I had made in this affair. I must say, that they are so strange and extraordinary, and such divers means used in their performance—that the accounts I hear in this garrison chill the soul and congeal the blood in one's veins. There is no way of hiding the misery and misfortune to which this Garrison is exposed. With the same truthfulness I must expose the fact, that I am positively certain from the reports of the Engineer Don Antonio Arredondo, as an eye-witness, that all the excesses committed by this Governor are strictly true as written you and certified to in a report from this Garrison.

The few Indians of our faith represent and express their lamentable sentiments on a paper written you, and sent through the Rev. Bishop of Micale. Other certificates of priests, military men, and private individuals of that Garrison, which I enclose add such scandalous excesses in the manner of living of that Governor that I cannot find decent words in which to express it. Some of these are signed by the same priests who wrote to Don Antonio Benavidos, and there are others, citing what the Governor has perpetrated on the Captain of Grenadiers, Don Felipe Iturricta, whom I sent there. Forgetting his merits and that he was a person of implicit confidence, whom I trusted for his unimpeachable conduct, they have placed him in prison under scandalous circumstances, intending to take from him the management of the troops over whom I placed him. He has been under the most rigorous guard, searching even his food, depriving him of the privilege of writing to ask for a hearing, accusing him of crimes and lack of obedience. They have no other course, in my opinion, than a pretext, as this Officer has fulfilled his duty with promptness and rectitude, showing only the ordinary precautions observed in the regiments for infinite reasons. The guards cannot be excused from the Barracks where the troop is stationed—which is one of the principal rudiments of military tactics—as well for safety as anything which might occur. The Captain insisted on maintaining these principles from which has arisen this trouble, and the assigning of the wrong conception of duty and want of obedience preferred against him. Of the same nature is the other charge: that he had defied the Governor. To this Captain Iturricta replied: if you were not the Governor you could not use such language to me—showing that he respected the office of Governor. The Governor does not seem to recognize the respect due to a man and Officer of standing and distinguished character, and let me add incidentally, placed here by me, as commandante of a detached body, to encourage and hold this fagged out Garrison. They should consider it an honor, for so distinguished a personage to accept this place, and so honorably discharge his duty. Your Majesty will understand all from the report of said Captain and the testimonials stating the circumstances. I also enclose a petition from the Captain in which he implores you to do him justice, a virtue so in keeping with your Royal heart, and not allow an officer of his standing to remain in disgrace. I can positively assure you, that had not the Captain and other Officers been true and faithful to their duty, they could have caused much trouble among the inhabitants of this Garrison, from this unjust act. Although I have reported all the abuses said to have been committed by the present Governor of Florida, and you should place some one of experience and good conduct in his place. I hope that your Majesty with your great experience, will pardon me for troubling you on the present occasion, and look unprejudiced into this affair. All that has been said of the matter, and all that I have been commanded in so important a trust—I am trying to investigate to the very root. Going cautiously, feeling my way, trying to right troubles without any scandal, so that I may send you the name of some worthy subject who can act *pro tem.* in that capacity—as, from all the information I have expounded it seems urgent you should remove this man, so as to restore the confidence your vassals have in your Majesty, and the responsibility I represent. The engineer, Don Antonio Arredondo, assures me no other expedient can be taken, while the present Governor is so engrossed in his own private interests, as you may infer from the last chapter.

Regarding the Barracks for lodging the hundred men, it is an evident fact, that but for the persistent effort of the Engineer Arredondo, they would have been returned to that Kingdom. All of which he reported to the Viceroy of Mexico that he might take the necessary precautions. Having disposed of the duty of having the Governor removed, I am doubtful of what will be best to do next toward your Majesty's interests, but I shall act as in my judgment seems best and as circumstances present themselves.

May God preserve you.

JUAN FRANCISCO HORCASITAS.

CHAPTER XV.

A. D. 1708-1723.

Letter from Francisco Carcoles y Martinez to his Majesty reports all possible measures taken to prevent the enemy from destroying this Province —The Indians, aided by the English who supply them with guns, ammunition, knives and pistols, come from the Indian villages bordering the Carolinas and carry off each day certain persons— Families and Christians taken off to be sold into slavery—More than ten thousand up to the present have disappeared—A treaty urged with the English of the Carolinas, else there will be a continuation of war and the spread of the Holy Gospel impeded — In a second letter the Governor gives an account of certain Friars who are getting up a dispute and lawsuit with the Priest of the Parish concerning the right and whose right to marry soldiers, Spaniards, Indians or mixed Indians—These disputes brought before the Governor to settle, who in turn refers them to his Majesty—Recommends the abolishing of all Heathen customs—By a Royal dispatch, A. D. 1721, the Governor of Florida is commanded to go in person to the Governor of the Carolinas and arrange with him the observance of the Treaty of Peace between the English and Spanish of those Provinces adjoining, which same was carried out as far as possible—A letter from the Governor, An-

tonio Bienavides, reports the sending of clothing and trinkets to pacify the Casiques and Chiefs of the Province of Appalachicola—Find the Indians restless and making preparations for war—English spreading dissatisfaction — A Council of War decides to send a vessel to Havana for arms, men and provisions in anticipation of troublous times.

THE GOVERNOR'S LETTER.

Your Lordship: A. D. 1708.

My principal care since assuming control as Governor has been to procure by all possible means to prevent the enemy from destroying at once this Province, and the few natives of it who have remained. When I took possession I called a meeting of the Board to discuss matters and we decided to· retire the troops from the town of Santa Fe, adding those of San Francisco and the infantry that was at the pass of Salamototo river, as I have already informed you on the 20th of November, 1706, so that with a larger force we might resist the enemy, and the citizens of this City feel some relief. I had built on the line a thick palisade, as I informed you. I have also organized a company of cavalry who should go about on the skirts, as they have done, to gather up stores and guard the carpenters and persons who go out to work cutting timber for the Royal buildings. This has not sufficed to stop the enemy from continuing their scalping and hostilities which are being constantly felt. They come from the Indian villages bordering on the Carolinas, aided by the English, who supply them with guns, ammunition, knives and pistols; at times they even accompany them, which strengthens and encourages them so that all the terra firma along the southern coast is desolate. And each day the number of families these Indians carry off is increased. The Christians have all disappeared, no doubt they have taken and sold them into slavery—more than ten or twelve thousand persons have gone. I have about three hundred with men, women and children. Even these are being carried away daily, when they go out to gather (guano) palmetto with which the Indians clothe themselves—and wild roots which they use for eating, not having sufficient with the Royal Rations which we daily allow them. Today they bring me an account of how they carried off ——— to Mica, who had gone out in search of roots—in all they have carried today twenty-eight persons, four of whom escaped and have brought the news. The fact of there being some capitulation of peace would be much added to the service of God and your Majesty by relieving us of these miserable Indians. All the natives from this Province are sold, imprisoned or detained in the Carolinas. If a treaty could be made with England to prevent the English in Carolina from supplying them with arms, ammunition, etc., for it is with this they make war against us, and the dexterity with which they use them is amazing—as though they had been brought up to their use. Unless such a treaty can be immediately reached, hostilities will continue, and in this America there will never be anything but war. And the English will always have the Indians on their side, as they protect them and furnish them with arms and ammunition, as they have done heretofore. Unless this treaty can be effected immediately, the best thing for us to do will be to abandon the place entirely, as you have suggested, before they desolate it. But as it is so important to the Crown and the vast importance and revenue which will and can be derived from it would make it deplorable to give it up now. Besides the great importance of spreading the Holy Gospel, as it is being done, has made me delay in giving you this necessary information.

May God guard you for many years as a true Christian. FRANCISCO CORCOLES Y MARTINEZ.

St. Augustine, Fla., January 14th, 1708.

LETTER OF THE GOVERNOR OF FLORIDA TO HIS MAJESTY.

Sire: A. D. 1708.

The continued coming of the enemy who took up quarters at San Francisco Garrison, caused the natives to retire to this Garrison to seek protection under the Royal arms. From the same fear, the palisade castle of Salamototo having been attacked, the few natives withdrew, running from the cruel ravages of these enemies. About eight or nine persons having called a meeting to discuss the matter of evacuating these Garrisons, the board decided that for the safety and better security of these natives it would be best to evacuate them. A more extensive account is given you in the testimony of each thing that I remit with this information, so that you may be well notified of the reasons for retiring from these two towns and others near them, that had already been deserted. We have assigned them land near by, in line of the cannon of this Royal Fort, and we are maintaining them and helping with the best we can at your expense and from the

Royal warehouses so that they may not perish until they can till the land and raise a crop to help support themselves, until things take a better turn. I hope your Majesty will approve and accept in good faith the step taken by the Board and that I am working and maintaining these natives for the best and greatest service of your Majesty. May God guard you as a Christian. FRANCISCO CORCOLES Y MARTINEZ.

St. Augustine, Fla., November 30th, 1708.

LETTER OF THE GOVERNOR OF FLORIDA TO HIS MAJESTY.

Sire: A. D. 1709.

I write to give you an account of the Friars of San Francisco. Fray Francisco, Teacher of the Gospel at Santa Maria de Guale, and the guardian of this Convent, Fray Martin de Molina, have been trying to get up lawsuits and have had disputes with the Pastor of this Parish, Don Pedro Lorenzo Acevido. These Friars are opposed to having the Pastor marry the soldiers or any Spaniard to the Indians or mixed Indians, wishing themselves to administer this and the other sacraments to them and their children. For this they have drawn up Autos and presented them to me that I might grant them justice. I referred them each to your Majesty, suggesting that they draw up their testimony and I am to reserve the right of informing you on the subject. I therefore call to your Royal attention how these law suits, occurring daily, only tend to disturb the peace. This is all done, because these Friars, to obtain the fee, wish now to administer these sacraments, which have been administered for the last thirty years by the parish priest of this parish, who has performed the marriage ceremony and had them watch (velar) from the fathers down to the grandchildren, without once interfering with the rights of these Friars to administer to their own people, the Indians in the towns they have charge of, and whose language they understand, and as is customary, if a soldier or any one wishes to marry an Indian or mixed Indian they must do so in the Parish and church to which the Indian belongs—thus, by degrees, leaving off all Heathen customs. Your Majesty after seeing the Autos and receiving this information will decide as he thinks best and most desirable for the good of all. May God preserve your Royal person that you may show justice.

FRANCISCO CORCOLES Y MARTINEZ.

St. Augustine, Fla., September 12th, 1709.

Sire: A. D. 1722.

By your Royal dispatch of May 25th of last year, 1721, you commanded me that taking advantage of the suspension of arms and the friendly relations I had observed with the English of the Carolinas since then; that your request at the Court of London had been granted. That under all these circumstances I should go in my official capacity to the Governor of Carolina and arrange with him to observe strictly the Treaty, that the vexation among the Indians who were allied to the two nations should cease. I immediately complied with your order and sent the Contador, Don Francisco Menendez, accompanied by other officials, from this Garrison, with the commission of having a firm agreement with the Governor of Carolina to make the Indians attached to his nation and to cease aggravating those with us, and thus live in peace and tranquility, pursuing agriculture. This peace being as important to one nation as the other, for, should war be declared, there would be no end to it. To this proposition and others as certified in the accompanying letter which I take this occasion of sending you, the Governor and Parliament of the Carolinas replied that they had received no such orders from the King of Great Britain, but that notwithstanding he would try to enforce peace during the suspension of arms. Immediately upon the arrival of Don F. Menendez in the Carolinas he was notified that the English had constructed a wooden fort on the tongue at the mouth of Talauje Province on your Majesty's territory, where, for many years the Indians and Guajas were settled and by reason of the siege this nation put on this Garrison, they had retired to where they still are. Don Francisco Menendez hearing this, considered it wrong for them to trespass upon your Territory, and so stated it to the Governor, and also that he feared harm would result from it. The reply given was: that the King of Great Britain had ordered them to strengthen his dominions with fortifications in any form they deemed expedient. Under different pretexts the "Contador" tried to have them show the order, but they refused to do so, saying it was sufficient that they said they had the order, and the Governor of Florida had nothing at all to do with it. From which I infer, your Lordship, that with the arrival of this new Governor in these colonies, not only will he complete the building of this Fort and settlement, but that he will also settle all the islands belonging to this jurisdiction, thus making the Carolinas impregnable and reducing this Garrison to a more lamentable state than it is in today on account of its easy access to the Indians who would immediately come to possess themselves of the ammunition and arms which it is the very heighth of their ambition to obtain. So Menendez learned that provision had been made by the English Government to equip this Colony, and they were awaiting, at any moment, vessels with supplies and arms. Then, at a moment's notice, they will invade this Castle, it being their great ambition, and the only and sole aim of it, to capture this Fort for the protection of the New England, and the great use they could make of it in capturing your Majesty's vessels coming through the Bahama Channel. In giving you this information I feel that I not only comply with my royal duty, but also discharge the debt to my conscience in showing you the danger of this Province. With this intelligence you can act as most agreeable and convenient. May God preserve your Royal personage for many years. ANTONIO BENAVIDOS.

St. Augustine, Fla., Apr. 21st, 1722.

The letter accompanying it:

St. Augustine, Fla., Feb. 11th, 1722.

Finding myself with an order from the King of Spain, my Lord and Master, for security with this and that government of reciprocal relations regarding the hostilities which on one and the other side has been completed, for the welfare of the Indians, I resolved to send to the Carolinas the "Contador" Don Francisco Menendez Marques, with other officials accompanying him, to confer with his Excellency and the Lords of Parliament for some agreement by which the annoyances of the infidel Indians toward those attached to our nation, might cease, and they be allowed to continue their agricultural pursuits without further disturbances and incentives—and not forgetting the agreement with Don Francisco Menendez Marques that during the suspension of arms, they try not to hostile the Indians of this Nation. That I, for my government, will keep them in subjection as I have done ever since the news of suspension of arms arrived, but that, if they should in any way fail in their agreement, they might rest assured that I shall take vengeance, and nothing shall deter me but their absolute subjection to our agreement. I shall make all necessary provision and watch with zeal, as I am fully persuaded that the keeping of this reciprocal agreement is the only foundation for tranquility and peace. Your Excellency will acknowledge receipt of this, and the agreement reached with Senor Menendez Marquez, that I may report to our King and Master.

ANTONIO BENAVIDOS.

TO THE KING FROM THE GOVERNOR OF FLORIDA.

Sire:

I place in your Royal hands the testimony of the letter written me by the Commandant whom I have in charge of the Garrison and Fort of San Marco, forwarded to him by Lieutenant Don Diego Pena who, by order, was sent to visit the Province of Apalachicola, with clothing and trinkets to gratify the Casiques and Chiefs. Both inform me that the Province of the Talepuses and others partial to the English of the

Carolinas, are restless and trying to destroy the nation of Arinaco who yield obedience to this government. That they are making all preparations for war, which from the evil designs we may soon expect. The number of the discontented is far in the ascendency of those who seem to be on our side, but in whom we can place no confidence, they being so deceitful. Then again, the fear they may entertain seeing that the English are mustering the Indians of so many nations and spreading dissatisfaction among them, against the Spaniards. The news given us by the Lieutenant that some of those we should and ought to trust have him detained in Colache from where he wrote this letter which, with the one from the commandant, I attach to these "Autos." Of the steps taken by the Council of War, whom I called together to discuss this matter, I will not send you testimony nor in any way trouble you. I shall only make known to your Royal intelligence that the Council of War decided to send a vessel to Havana with letters to the Governor of that place, that he might aid us in sending provisions, arms and men—the latter to land at some point further down and, taking horses, make their way in by land. The enemy may already have the place blockaded. Should you decide that this plan ought not to be carried out I am willing to sacrifice my life to have the disturbances among these Nations cease, and that all under control of this Government should live in peace, without any of the prejudices of those who disturb them. Besides, as is written in the Holy Gospel, "we will ravish the enemy, punish and destroy them." But, my Lord, the condition of this garrison is such that it will be impossible for us to hold out for any

Old St. Augustine 173

length of time. The rapidity with which they are gathering and preparing indicates we are to have serious and trying times. Ever since 1702 our forces have been falling off, and we are weak. In giving you this information I am stating truths and fulfill my duty. Act as in your judgment with the aid of God is best. ANTONIO BIENAVIDOS.

St. Augustine, Fla., August 18th, 1723.

CHAPTER XVI.

A. D. 1736-1739.

In a letter to his Majesty Governor Senor Montiano says it is reported that Don Diego Oglethorpe has said openly "that should he receive orders from his Government to fix the boundary limits between the Spanish possessions and the Carolinas he would so delay the execution that there should never be a sign of these limits"—Montiano thinks it would be wise for such a gentleman to be removed as it can never be possible to discuss questions of importance with him—In A. D. 1738 the same Governor reports the result of a trip of investigation by one Juan Ygnacio de los Reyes, an Indian—Under the pretext of giving himself up from having killed an Indian, he gains much information concerning the English, their plans against the Spanish, misleading the English as to the strength, numbers and condition of Spanish fortifications, finally escaping under pretext of hunting — Returns with valuable information to the Spanish—Statement of what has been ordered regarding the aid to Florida Provinces, the dislodging of the enemy from certain settlements on its territory, since its government up to 1674— Dispatch of 1675 commands that if the negro slaves sent to Havana have not already been sold, they shall be sent to Florida, to be put to work on

Old St. Augustine

the construction of the Castle to relieve the Indians.

LETTER FOR HIS MAJESTY FROM THE GOVERNOR OF FLORIDA, SENOR MONTIANO.

My Lord:

In a letter of the 28th of March of this year, you were kind enough to acknowledge receipt of my letter of August 14th of last year, in which I reported that Don Diego Oglethorpe, Commander of the English colonies, had said openly that although he should receive orders from his King and Court to fix the boundary limits between this government's possessions and those of the Carolinas, he would delay the execution of it, so that there should never be a sign of these limits, and they must bear this always in mind, for whatever might present itself. With this intelligence it would be well to relieve these Colonies of such a man, because on questions of importance upon any occurrence which should need discussion, it would be exceedingly troublesome to manage a gentleman who even refuses to answer my former letters. This is all I can say on the subject—placing it before your Sovereign Majesty to whom God grant many years.

MANUEL MONTIANO.

St. Augustine, Fla., August 11th, 1736.

A. D. 1738.

Information given by the Indian, Juan Ygnacio de los Reyes, of the Iquaha Nation, one of the neighbors of the town of Pocotalaca in the immediate vicinity of this Garrison. He says: That he left under my orders on the 4th of July of this year to go to the neighboring English colony, and ascertain by as many ways and artifices as he could, their intentions, the state or condition they are in, and everything. He took a small canoe at the Fort of Picolata and went down that river and sailed through the mouth of the Sarabai, going as far as the Fort of San Pedro, which belongs to the English, meditating upon what scheme he should take to gain all this information, and not go about hiding and endangering his life needlessly. He thought of delivering himself up, as he did, pretending that he had killed an Indian here, and was fleeing not to be hung; that he was seeking protection from them. On learning this he was favorably received, and could see a Fort which was square and stockaded with two pieces and a cannon looking seaward; in it was a detachment of twenty soldiers more or less, there is no neighborhood, and saw but four houses before coming to the Fort or Stockade; a few laborers planting corn; that the soldiers who are there are from a small vessel or Piroque of war, intended to seek the mouths of rivers; that from this Fort of San Pedro he was taken by two soldiers to the Bar of Ballenas, that is where the first place called San Andres is, there he saw a number of soldiers drilling with spears, and although he did not then know their exact number, he afterwards learned in St. Simons from Lieutenant-Colonel Cochran that there were three hundred; that he there saw a number of houses, newly built and close together as in Havana, a number of English women, wives of the soldiers, but he could not tell the number of houses in the place; that there is also a square Fort, with four cannon, towards the sea, and on the other side he could not see; that there were small guard houses around it. He could not see if they had artillery, because they would not allow him too near; that from here to the sea inland by the Bay there is a thick palisade of earth with a parapet and at the extreme end there is a wharf and they told him that there they had flints for the Spaniards, and they keep a launch ready and armed so that at any moment of the day or night she can be used. She is manned with sixteen men. They carried him to St. Simons to the presence of Colonel Cochran. Immediately upon his arrival there, they sent six soldiers with bayonets to escort him to the Colonel's house. He was asked where he was going, he replied to seek protection and favor from them; he had killed an Indian in St. Augustine. Colonel Cochran extended his hand to him, but when he went to take it he only gave him one finger. He was asked about the Armada which was to encounter them; how many vessels and men it brought. He told them he had not seen it, but had heard there were a hundred vessels with more than 4,000 men. and that the Governor of St. Augutine had told them to return, that he did not wish to hurt the English. He was asked how many troops were in this Garrison—he replied that there used to be four companies of one hundred soldiers on horse, but that recently five more companies of one hundred men each had arrived. They then asked if there was much silver in Florida. He replied: Yes, as there were so many soldiers, money flowed freely. Then Colonel Cochran told him all that would soon belong to the King of Great Britain. He was then asked about the Castle and Garrison. He told them the Castle had one hundred and sixty cannons so large he could not reach around them; the Garrison had twelve bulwarks with ten cannon each. To which Colonel Cochran told him: Well, see here; when you hear that General Oglethorpe, whom I am expecting with seven thousand men, has arrived, then you will see me place a vessel of war at the mouth of the Bar, and prevent any food from entering Florida. On the keys I shall place others and no one shall enter Havana, expressing himself in such a way as to say that the King of England would gain more by taking Florida than Gibraltar; that while that was advantageous, this would yield them a great deal more. This conversation was continued, asking if the Castle could be reached if there was water inside, to all of which he told them it was impossible. Speaking of the Governor, he asked for a grape arbor he had in his house, said to yield great quantities of grapes. He told them the Governor was a saintly man, and that while he knew him to be so good, he could not help but flee from the punishment he knew he deserved for killing the Indian, because the Governor was also a just man. That it was true he had a grape arbor producing large quantities of grapes. Colonel Cochran then said: Very well, within one or two years we will make our wine and whiskey there. He says that day and night he never tired asking about Florida; that now they were fortifying to afterwards come and take it; that in St. Simons he had three hundred troops, as many more in San Andres and Sabanato. He had brought these to take Florida, but hearing of the Spanish Armada, they had desisted and sent for seven thousand more men, whom Oglethorpe would bring, and upon the arrival of this Commander in less than two months they would gather 506,000 Indians; that he would make his entrance by the river St. Johns in schooners and small vessels and disembark at a place some seven leagues distant from Florida, where they had two small ports. These Juan Ygnacio saw with his own eyes, where they have the men they were drillng at San Andres. That in St. Simons he saw ten squares with ten houses and seventy houses in six squares, the other four squares were not completed. That in each of the houses they lodged six soldiers. That he also saw a Fort with fifteen cannon, and as it was in a bad condition, they were making brick to rebuild it. That going out to hunt, he came near the house of "Frederico" distant from St. Simons three leagues more or less. The English would not allow him to enter there, but turned him back to St. Simons. That about one league from this place he saw a vessel called the Mamal, and there he saw them building six large houses in which they had fifty men, that they had large timber works. This he knows positively, having been there twice. That Cochran and another Englishman whom he thinks they call William Houston, he overheard say that they had offered the Indians fifty dollars for every Spanish scalp they killed, black or white, or Christian Indian, any one partial to Spain. That his escape to return was accomplished in the following manner: That one Thursday at ten o'clock in the morning he told Cochran that he was going hunting, if he found no game he would remain over night and fish, returning the next day; he allowed him to go; taking advantage of the occasion he took his canoe and sailed along the rivers until Friday morning, when he got on terra firma, leaving his canoe he walked two days in the direction of the sunset, then crossed over the land and at the end of ten days he was on the St. Johns river where he found the launch from this Garrison, which is there on guard. Having called and taken his shirt for a flag, they went and brought him over. The same day he started for this place where he arrived at twelve o'clock at night and gave the information as I send it.

MANUEL MONTIANO.

St. Augustine, Fla., Aug. 20th, 1738.

By a Cedula of June 20th, 1671, the Viceroy of New Spain has been ordered to communicate with the Governor of Florida, hoping that through his zeal much can be accomplished in the cause of the English, preventing them from getting a strong foothold so near the mouth of the river St. Elena, which would be prejudicial to our interests. Therefore the Viceroy is requested to give all the aid required. As to the proposed fortification to this Port for its defense, do what is necessary to defend the Province and communicate also with the Viceroy whom I have commanded to try and give all the assistance possible, always bearing in mind not to violate the laws of the capitulation of peace. The Governor of Havana being nearest to Florida was also commanded to communicate with the Governor of Florida and render all the aid and assistance possible in the dislodging of the English from the river St. Elena, who if remaining in said place would cause much trouble. The Governor of Florida must also keep him informed of the state of affairs. In a letter dated April, 1671, the

Viceroy Marquez de Mancera gives an account of the aid sent to the Garrison of St. Augustine in accordance with Cedula received. The papers showing that this aid had been received and approved by the Council of War, accompanying this letter, which also states the order given the Governor of New Spain to be very careful in keeping a continual correspondence with the Governor of Florida, send supplies promptly, and notify the Viceroy of all that occurs. Act in every way for the best security of that Garrison, using the greatest diligence in its fortification and defense, being as I understand of such importance. State what steps have been taken in regard to the fortification that was to be built, and to which reference is made in this dispatch to the Governor Manuel Cendovia and if the supplies of the soldiers and provisions to begin the work have arrived.

By Cedula of May 9th it was again commanded the Viceroy, calling his special attention to it, that he must aid and supply this Garrison that it may be in readiness for any emergency which may arrive. By another Cedula the Governor of Florida was to inform the inhabitants of that Fort, find out if they had their full quota for its defense, or if they found it necessary to increase the number on account of the new settlement of English sixty miles north. How long they had been there, and if they were sufficiently provided to dislodge the English, which information must be given so as to provide all and anything that is necessary. The Governor represented that in the past, the number of infantry in the Garrison was three hundred in which were included men of different trades, forty missionary priests without whom the number was not complete, adding that the total number was three hundred. When the news of the looting by the English arrived they immediately sent to the Viceroy of New Spain to send five hundred men to increase the infantry, appealing to Mexico for more men to complete the number, they replied that they had sent assistance to other Garrisons where they were watching and had to have supplies and artillery, so that the War Department had provided all it could. But to send to Havana and have the Governor of that Post to act as he had been commanded and send with the utmost speed the necessary defense for that Garrison. That the Viceroy had been notified to order the Royal officers of Mexico to increase the supplies of Florida each year by forty-three recruits, so that there should never be less than three hundred and ninety in quarters. A Notice of which was sent the Governor of Florida that he might keep them informed of its fulfilment. To pay special care and vigilance to the Province, having it well defended against accident from the enemy entering, they could instantly banish and punish them. The Governor of Florida also made known the great want of artillery, having consulted with the War Department that same date, the War Department ordered the Viceroy of New Spain and Governor of Havana each to send without delay two pieces of bronze artillery at the same time they had sent an order to the contracting house in Sevilla to send other pieces that were in that City on the first occasion and also the two hundred arms asked for, that the Garrison may not be without the means of defense and safety. To keep the infantry under good discipline and that the Governor

Old St. Augustine 183

place himself in communication with the Viceroy and the Governor of Havana to see that they send him four pieces of artillery. The Florida Governor gave an account in this letter also, of having formed a cavalry company and a military company enlisting in them all who were able, old men and boys not yet of age, his own sons among them. This he did for the greater safety of the place against the enemy. He was giving the utmost zeal and care to his duties. In a letter of 1674 the Sergeant-Major acting as Governor of the Province of Florida, states that a vessel had arrived at that Port and they had received four pieces of artillery and other ammunition from the contracting house in Sevilla, that with this and the artillery that was to come from Havana and New Spain, these would be sufficient for the defense of the Garrison. By a dispatch of 1674 thanks were sent the Archbishop, Viceroy, for having sent to Florida all the supplies due that Garrison. It was sent that it might leave on the fleet passing Vera Cruz for Spain.

By another dispatch the Governor, Pablo Ita Salazar, was recommended that he apply himself with much zeal in perfecting the fortification of the Royal Fort being built in that City and that it be accomplished in a manner for the best safety of the Province. By Cedula of 1675 the Sergeant-Major Don Nicolas Ponce de Leon, in reply to a letter of his, and attentive to an order sent the Governor of Cuba, that if the negro slaves sent to Havana had not already been sold, he should send immediately upon their arrival fifty of them to Florida, where they should be put to work on the Castle under construction. The Indians who served as peons were not strong and their people were much opposed to their leaving the planting of corn which is the sustenance of their families. And the Governor was ordered upon their arrival in Florida to apply them to this work and relieve the Indians and to finish the construction as quickly as possible.

CHAPTER XVII.

A. D. 1741-1743.

Conduct of the Christians worse than the heathen— Soldiers guarded while they are cuttng timber to repair the Fort—The Castle in a tumble-down condition—The Garrison to be maintained for the propagation of the Holy Gospel, and to shelter the workers of the Apostolic faith—A paper of representation to his Majesty concerning the properties belonging to the Treasurer, Don Francisco Menendez, deceased, left by will to the Royal Treasury —The pressing need of the Infantry of this Garrison; it having no capital, the property should be sold at public auction and proceeds go to restore back pay of troops to alleviate suffering, hunger and need for clothing, instead of being used for a hospital as per the King's desire—A letter from Governor Manuel Montiano informs his Majesty of fourteen English vessels anchored off the Bar of this Port—Six Spanish galleys sent to meet them at which the enemy retires.

Sire: A. D. 1741.

By the dispatches which, on this occasion, I send you duplicates as well as the original, you and your Royal and Supreme Council of the Indias will see the royal and Supreme Council of the Indias will see the condition of this Port. The continued watch and worry I have. The continuous watch by day and night of the Infantry to repulse the hostilities of these enemies. The heathen not being as bad as the Christians who have risen and commit the most bloody deeds upon all those whom they catch, carrying off Indians as well as soldiers prisoners to the Carolinas, where they sell them into bondage. For the execution of this they have a different set of soldiers stationed at the terminus of all the roads leading to this Garrison. I am forced to send out troops on foot and horse to accompany any party going out to fell and saw timber for the much needed repairs of the ramparts, gather wood, coal, etc. I began these repairs as soon as I took possession, otherwise the whole thing would have been demolished and left us with no defense whatsoever. These repairs cannot last long, for the reasons I have already repeatedly informed you, and lastly, the great need the Royal Troops have of rebuilding the ramparts, quarters, warehouses and roofs that they may stay in at all. To save you such enormous expense as each day occurs, it will be necessary to fortify the place at once, because with the English in such close proximity as the Carolinas, this Port is in the greatest danger of being lost, as the troops are defenseless and needy as you have been repeatedly informed, and you have given such stringent orders that the Viceroy should supply all that is needed for the expulsion of these English, and for which I have done my part far as possible, as you will see from the consultation I had with him on the 10th of April of this year, an account of which I rendered your Majesty. Notwithstanding the risk of encountering these enemies, no occasion is lost of going out to find what is needed and necessary for the preservation and defense of the Port. Cutting and sawing timber for the stables and artillery, the most important things—the soliciting of supplies that we may not be in want as the entire Garrison and neighborhood depend entirely upon the Royal Warehouses for their sustenance, as I long ago informed you on the 24th of March. I am hourly awaiting my successor, to whom I shall give all needed instruction regarding the defense of this Port from the enemy. I have decided to surrender as far as possible the execution of the repairs I have mentioned that he may apply all that he gets to the service of the two Majesties; that this Garrison may be maintained for the propagation and extension of the Holy Gospel, as has been done by the good Catholics, the Kings, your predecessors of a hundred and sixty years, at such enormous expense with no other interest than to shelter with these arms the Workers of the Apostolic faith to the greater honor and glory of God. May He preserve your Majesty.

FRANCISCO CORCOLES Y MARTINEZ.

St. Augustine, Fla., December 11th, 1741.

REPRESENTATION.

1743.

The Officers of the Royal Treasury of this Garrison, at the most convenient time and without prejudice to the definite appeal and protests made in favor of the same Royal Treasury, represent to your Highness that in view of this Post having more than seven hundred men, re-enforcement over and above the troops of its Garrison. That with the demise of Don Francisco Menendez Marquez, Auditor who was, of these same

Royal Coffers, your Highness has thought that the houses occupied by him as residence, and all the balance of his property to which he made the King his sole and only heir, should be dedicated to the use of hospitals to serve these same troops of the infantry of this Garrison when occasion offers, on account of the war. Before your Highness determines to take this step, it becomes indispensable that we should expose the fact to you that we cannot consent to have the abovementioned houses assigned to any such uses for the following reasons:

First, because in his will Don Francisco Menendez Marquez himself declares that, not being able from the balance of his accounts to satisfy the Royal Treasury, he understood directly that it became compulsory for him to ease his conscience that he should name the King his sole and only heir. From this is deduced that all property known as that of Don Francisco Menendez is, with legitimate title, the property of the Royal Treasury. Not having the authority to sell these without an order from your Majesty, it is consistent that we who are his executors and lack the Royal permit to determine what disposition to make of it resist the intention and thought your Highness has formed of the use of the above mentioned houses and balance of property of the aforementioned gentleman. It seemed to us that in all fairness and justice they should be closed out at public auction and the proceeds thereof distributed among the Infantry of this Garrison; because this Garrison has no capital of its own, it follows that the legitimate creditors to the property are these same troops. The Royal Treasury is under obligation to restore to the Infantry the back pay due them, and never better than now, that they lack clothing and are perishing, should aid come at a more opportune time, and it could be done with the proceeds of this property, lessening the obligation of the Royal Treasury that amount.

Second: Your Highness can have no conception of the increased suffering occasioned by the war. The curing of the wounded soldiers and sailors who have been in this Post for over two years, there being no capital to apply to the indispensable expense of medical attendance for this purpose, it is easy to understand that the situation is burdened by heavy expenses, and to make it clearer, up to the present date no provision has been made to cover the cost of the many works of fortification in this Post and on the bar of Matanzas to defend them against the continued attacks of our enemy, and for the multitude of Indians who have attached themselves to us with so much firmness and friendship, who forgetting us, and the word given to your Highness of remaining neutral in the actual war between ourselves and the English, and of the liberality of the King who orders them always to be treated with so much kindness and affection when they come.

In a letter of September 15th of last year we explained to your Majesty how fourteen English vessels had anchored off the bar of this Port, coming prepared and perfectly sure they could disembark and take possession. The six galleys of your Majesty met them, and notwithstanding their continued firing they made them retire. We await and naturally expect them to return and try to carry out their intentions. And therefore, your Majesty's service is as vigilant as possible to be on the alert to prevent it. It has been a great pleasure and satisfaction to us to inform your Majesty of the good results obtained by the efforts of your six galleys in expelling the enemy. We are watching closely along the coast of this Province for any other design they may have of entering. God preserve you. MANUEL MONTIANO.

El Prado, March 30th, 1743.

Old St. Augustine

CHAPTER XVIII.
A. D. 1770-1771.

A letter of resolution to his Majesty in respect to a letter of appeal made to the Governor and the Bishop of Havana asking for patent and Holy oil to administer baptism and extreme unction to the Catholic families taken from the Island of Minorca by the English—These families bringing with them one Don Pedro Campos, Doctor of Sacred Theology, as a Parish Priest, and Don Bartolome Casanovas, of the St. Augustine order, Vicar— These same claiming to have received their appointment from the Supreme Pontificate, not knowing to which Bishop this jurisdiction of Florida belonged—At the end of three years to appear in writing to the Prelate of the Apostolic choir of that Diocese—This letter sent secretly by a fisherman—In order that a thorough investigation may be made, the matter is referred to his Royal Highness—Letter of the Archbishop of Valencia concerning same—Letter of the Bishop of Cuba to his Majesty, in which he expresses gratification over the zeal his Highness has shown concerning this matter—Advises that these privileges be conferred upon Dr. Pedro Campos and Pedro Casanovas— Letter of the Bishop of Minorca giving information concerning the exporting of these families from the Island of Minorca by the English.

LETTER OF RESOLUTION.

Sire: A. D. 1770.

By order of his Majesty I sent the Knight of the Order, Fray Don Julian de Arriaga, with papers of February 27th of this year, to the Governor of Havana, and documents which treat especially of the appeal made to the Bishop of that diocese, asking him for patent and Holy oil to administer baptism and extreme unction to the Catholic families who were taken from Minorca, to colonize the territory in Florida, belonging to the English, so that it may be recognized and consulted in the Council whatever may come up on this subject. The proclaimed Governor Don Antonio Bucareli y Ursna give an account referring to the above mentioned documents. He states that he received a letter addressed to the Bishop of that diocese by one of the passing fish boats on its way to the northern coast for the fisheries. That immediately upon its receipt, he made returns of a copy of it, and its entire sentiment, which he forwarded. From the appearance of its contents, the subject treated, in their judgment it seemed proper to lay the whole matter before your Majesty, including a copy of the aforementioned letter. that you might decide what was most agreeable to your Royal pleasure. In the already mentioned letter signed it seems by Don Pedro Campos, Doctor of Sacred Theology, dated from Mosquito on the 20th of October of 1769, the prelate lays before the public the fact that one year previous Mr. Andrew Turnbull, an Englishman, had taken from the Island of Minorca about 1300 persons to colonize Florida, for whom he was appointed Par-

Old St. Augustine 193

ish Priest and Don Bartolome Casanovas, of the St. Augustine order, Vicar of said jurisdiction. They had received their appointment from the Supreme Pontificate, not knowing to which Bishop this jurisdiction of Florida belonged, but it was their duty to appear by writing before the expiration of three years to the Prelate of the Apostolic chair in that diocese. That both of them are natives of Minorca, which Island was temporarily subject to the King of Great Britain and spiritually to the Bishop of Minorca. That he had studied philosophy and theology, received all the orders, been one of the governing body and Vicar. This last office he had held for twelve years in Minorca. Preached during several Lents, as had also Padre Casanovas. For all these reasons he begs that he be sent a patent of Parochial Priest and one of Vicar to Fray Casanovas. He also asks for some of the Holy Oil used in baptism and extreme unction. That all these be sent him by the same secret means of the fishermen for the spiritual aid and advancement of those Catholic people.

Successively the same Knight of the Order sent another paper and testimony to the Bishop of Cuba, Don Santiago Echevarria, saying that the dispatch or expedient sent belonged to the Council. With the order of February 27th referring to the solicitude felt by that Vicar and Parish Priest for the families who had been transported from Minorca, so that they might be united to this tribunal which could proceed to recognize them as stated in the prepared information. In it the same prelate, Don Julian Arriaga, of the diocese, states that at the same time he had full knowledge of the letter of Dr. Campos, the Governor passed a bill considering it not worthy of his consideration and not recognizing the legitimacy of the letter of the pretendent nor his pontifical jurisdiction. Affirming that the testimony was of little value or belief. The simple say so of a letter. The class of foreigners who lived among heretics, diminished their estimation of the Holy Oil, finally that he considered it absolutely necessary to lay the whole matter before your Majesty. Considering each clause of the letter, he deemed that it should be answered by the minister, arranging all according to his judgment and resolution to be made known, so that hereafter he may know how to proceed in similar cases. The Council, in view of the referred report, placed it before the Judge, whose original answer is in the hands of your Royal Highness confirming the opinion it contains and placing before your Royal consideration that the judgment found by the Bishop of Cuba has been very prudent, that he has worked with wise precaution, because truly the contents of Dr. Campos' letter are very delicate, and one should be cautious in being influenced by a weak letter entrusted to uncertain fishermen. That at all events it lacks the necessary antecedents required for an affair of less importance. That the foundation should be the legitimizing of the persons referred to by the Priest and the Fray Casanova. The claims with which they passed to Florida in company with the families from Minorca and the jurisdiction they assure us to have received from the Supreme Pontificate. Nothing of this has been sent in document form, nor promised to be sent in such form, ignoring also whether the families from said Island taken out by the English were Catholics, and if they had passed into Florida as such and with the freedom of enforcing their religion. That Catholics, permanent residents of Florida, should ask spiritual aid of the Bishop of Cuba, is perfectly proper, because, before the occupation of the English, Mosquito was under his jurisdiction. Neither should sacred things be exposed to the scorn and ridicule of heretics, nor should it be badly administered. The secret manner in which Dr. Campos seeks this aid, so very queer, because if the families from Minorca are Catholic and were transported as such to Florida with the free privilege of their religion, as is seen by their efforts in bringing with them a Parish Priest and Vicar. The English would certainly not oppose them in publicly asking for and having all that is required by these same Catholics for administering the sacraments, education of the masses, and spiritual good of their souls. All this makes it indispensable that we should have a thorough knowledge and investigation of these affairs by other means before we can decide on this matter with any certainty. To which is added that by the article eleven of the Treaty of Peace adjusted on the 13th of July of the year 1713, in which was ceded to the crown of Great Britain the Island of Minorca, (among other things) promised by his British Majesty was that the inhabitants of the said Island should enjoy in all safety and peacefulness all the honors and privileges of the Roman Catholic religion, and also that for the preservation of this religion they should take all measures which did not appear exposed to the Government of Sevilla and laws of Great Britain. Thus it seems to the Council that your Minister in Rome should be appointed to investigate the matter with the greatest solicitude, because if the Catholics of the above mentioned Island of Minorca, transported by the English in the year 1768 (as we deduce from Dr. Campos' letter), have made an appeal to the Apostolic Secretary in order to carry with them their own Pastor, and if his Holiness has named in the capacity of the Parish Priest and Vicar the referred to Don Pedro Campos and Don Bartolome Casanova of the St. Augustine Order, and such jurisdiction assigned to them.

Being informed as briefly and clearly as possible, extend an order to the Captain-General of the Island of Minorca and to the Bishop of that Diocese that they may separately inform if they know of the exportation of the families of Minorca by the English to populate Florida. If the declared families were Catholic, and if the Prelates lived and behaved as priests; if they passed over here with the understanding that they had free use of their religion, if Dr. Campos and Pedro Casanova were elected as Parish Priest and Vicar of them. What is the character and circumstances of these two subjects, and if on accepting they gave notice and obtained permission of that minister and that prelate. In the meanwhile if the steps have been taken, it is imperative that the Governor of Havana and the Bishop of Cuba be given to understand that the prudent steps taken by them was exactly and perfectly agreeable to your Majesty. Their determination and your agreeing with it perfectly as though they had anticipated your resolution on the present subject. That without appearing in it, the Bishop should try by all means available to investige the manner of practising the Catholic re-

Old St. Augustine 197

ligion by these Minorcans in Florida. The position of Dr. Campos and Fray Casanova who are supposed to be Parish Priest and Vicar of the Catholic portion of the settlement. Let a similar order be given the Governor so as to advance as speedily as possible with the news, giving information of the results of the search that your Majesty may decide on what is most agreeable to your Royal Highness.

Madrid, Sept. 27th, 1770.

LETTER OF THE ARCHBISHOP OF VALENCIA.

My Dear Sir:

Having formed the corresponding petition, begging for an extension of the privileges granted Don Pedro Campos and Pedro Bartolome Casanovas, I also asked the Pope in the name of his Royal Majesty to grant these ministers all privileges in their spiritual management, as requested by his Majesty.

Your Lordship notified me as seems quite proper the time to investigate concerning these privileges, he being one of the supervisors at the tribunal of the Holy Office, he immediately accomplished what was asked by sending to his Holiness at the instigation of Monsenor Autoville, Assessor of said Tribunal, who spoke favorably of helping them with his influence, as he did, and you will see by the enclosed letter of Saturday sent by Senor Zelada. He informs me that his Holiness extends to them the privileges for a term of twenty years and inquires of me if I have attended to the balance of the communications soliciting greater privileges for these Ecclesiastics, enclosing for my instruction the printed pamphlet of privileges granted the Bishop of Cuba, where he facilitates the authentic open mandate. Seeming to me to be agreeable and satisfactory to the King, I replied that he should ask these privileges and notify me, as he has done, and which I send you, hoping they will deserve your approval and the pleasure of his Majesty. I take this occasion of placing myself at your disposal, and may God grant you a long life is the wish of

THE BISHOP OF VALENCIA.

Trascati, August 28th, 1771.

LETTER OF THE BISHOP OF CUBA.

Sire:

I have had the honor of receiving the Royal Cedule of your Majesty dated in Idelfonso 16th of August, of this year, in reply to my letter of February 19th. You condescend to enclose me a copy of what the Rev. Bishop of Minorca has written regarding the Catholic families who were taken from Minorca to establish themselves in the English territory of Florida, called Mosquito, and a literal copy of the privileges granted by the Apostolic See to the Parish Priest and Vicar of them.

You order me that in the use of peculiar privileges and delegated in consequence of the subordination under which these Presbyters declare themselves. I should grant them the titles they ask of parochial and assistant in the most approved form under the present state of affairs—to furnish them with the Holy Oil as long as there should be no reason for withholding it, and take entire care of those faithful, governing them by means of these ministers, and taking as many pre-

Old St. Augustine 199

cautions as I consider proper to the preservation of the faith, availing myself in case of need of the Governor and Captain-General of this Island. Your Majesty advises me of the official letters addressed by the Secretary of State to the Court of London, representing clearly what was said by the Bishop of Minorca, and also the result of the solicitation which by your order has aided the Rev. Archbishop of Valencia with his Holiness, in obtaining from him an extension of the privileges granted these Ecclesiastics extend even beyond mine—and it is well and needed for the spiritual good of this Catholic portion. Have the goodness to permit me to express the sweet commotion my soul has felt at seeing the proper zeal on the part of your Majesty, and the interest you take in extending the Kingdom of Christ over all the world. This example must influence the Pastors, as we have the honor of rendering homage to so great and Catholic a Monarch.

As to the instructions of your Sovereign Majesty that I should communicate your resolutions to the Marquez de la Torre, the new Governor and Captain-General of this city and Island, I did not have to encourage his zeal in the affair. Full of the greatest energy in the service of God and your Majesty, he immediately fitted up a vessel which, under the pretext of fishing along the coast of Florida, should approach Mosquito Inlet and deliver to Dr. Pedro Campos, through safe hands, the two titles, for himself that of Parish Priest and Vicar for his companion, Pedro Casanovas—a delegation of various privileges I have considered advisable for the spiritual good of that Diocese under its dangerous constitution. A casket containing three vessels of the Holy Oil needed, and two assistants for the divine worship, all of which I offer up to the service of God.

These documents I place at the foot of your throne. By them you will see how I have written to these Ministers inspiring them with a spirit of gratitude. I encourage and sustain them to carry out their good enterprise, exacting a report under pretext of aiding them in their spiritual emergencies. The moment I obtain them I shall send to your Majesty all the light I obtain on the subject. I shall be on the lookout to consult the books used by these Religious men, and aid them in all that is needed for the reasonable administration of the sacraments and health of their souls. Judging by the measures I have taken of their delegation they will scarcely need the extension of the first words of the Holy Chair. On the arrival of these, I shall take other means more suitable to these circumstances, and in all shall try to carry out the real intentions your Majesty has deemed proper to state to me and nothing will be more gratifying than to ascertain them through my fidelity to God, who I hope will preserve you for many years.

Havana, December 14th, 1771.

LETTER OF THE BISHOP OF MINORCA.

My Dear Sir:

On date of October 27th just passed and by order of your Majesty, on the occasion of a representation made you by common accord by the Bishop and Governor of Havana, I was commissioned by Don Tomas Melio, predecessor of your Majesty's, to give any infor-

Old St. Augustine 201

mation I could regarding the exporting of the families from the Island of Minorca by the English to colonize Florida. If these families were Catholics and if Dr. Pedro Campos and Padre Bartolome Casanovas, who accompanied them, had been elected for that purpose, their character and circumstances and if for the acceptance of this commission they notified me and obtained my license.

It seems suitable to my ministry to give a categorical reply to what has been asked, the impediments imposed on my jurisdiction by the Governor of said Island when the exportation was carried into effect, with me to the extent of opening my private letters, suspecting others might be enclosed in them for me. This deprived me of all news regarding the exportation, which by means of some who came from said Islands brought me news of my Vicar-General by word of mouth, it being impossible to write under the circumstances, that the families were all Catholics and passed over with the free use of their religion having accompanied them two Ecclesiastics to serve as Parochial Priests, and I am persuaded they were the same who gave rise to the representation. During the opposition of that Governor to the exercise of my authority I many times resorted to carry from the Island to the Court, to men who were worthy to protect the benignity of our Catholic religion with messages to your Ambassador at the Court and at my instigation they were placed at your Royal feet by the Marquez of Grimalde with whose powerful help and meditation we finally obtained a hearing of the private Council of the King of Great Britain which took place on last June, when a Decree was sent stating that no state, and I have placed myself in communication with the Vicar to whom I have written that without loss of time he informed me of all that had occurred in the exportation, how executed, the circumstances of the two Ecclesiastics and if they went with this permission, and all else conducive to a satisfactory reply. This I will fulfill immediately I receive a reply. In the meantime the exportation being undoubtedly public and notorious, also that it was occasioned by the want and suffering endured in that Island by many families on account of poor crops for several consecutive years which obliged me to grant dispensation from the eating of lactenacious food and meat on prohibited days. Most of the families who went to Florida had come to this Island to colonize the unhappy city of Aludia, and if I rightly understand, I do not doubt but that some went to Cierra Morena or other places in Spain, from the manner in which the Vicar-General communicated to me the exportation, I doubt if the Ecclesiastics went with his permission, he would only have allowed and tolerated it for the good of the religion and not to irritate the Governor more by reports which, when I first arrived on this Island, he gave me of all the Ecclesiastics. It results that Dr. Campos was a good and laborious Priest, devoted strictly to his ministerial duties, and had been Vicar for some years. That he was Vicar of a village of that Island. This is confirmed by several persons of Minorca who, in this unsettled state, are still here, and although some of the clergy do not give such good reports, those they have given of his conduct are not bad, but being obliged to state all that I understood in this city regarding the exportation, I am assured by several

Old St. Augustine

persons that bad news is being spread of the unhappiness in which these families live, their disgust with the country where there is nothing but hard labor and want, in place of the happiness and riches they had been promised by the English, and what is worse, that they themselves (without stating the reason) had assassinated the said Clergyman who had accompanied them. This is all I can tell you at present, until I have a reply for the worse from my Vicar-General of Minorca. In the meantime I take this occasion to congratulate your Majesty upon your new destiny and after my services praying God may grant you long life. BISHOP OF MINORCA.

Palma, February 5th, 1771.

CHAPTER XIX.

A. D. 1771.

The opinion of the Judge, after having examined the different letters from the Bishops and those in authority connected therewith and after making thorough investigation into this matter concerning the granting of the patent and graces asked for by these Priests of the Minorcan families of the English colony of Florida—The Bishop of Cuba for the Council to Dr. Don Pedro Campos and the Rev. Father Bartolome Casanovas, extends to these Priests the title of Parish Priest and Vicar—Also sends a box containing three flasks of Sacred Oil—Hopes soon to be able to send a more extended prorogation of other powers—This grace having been solicited by the King from the Court of Rome—Asks for a more extended report of the number of families and condition of the congregation.

The Judge has seen a letter of the Rev. Archbishop of Valencia, Minister of his Majesty, in the Court of Rome, dated Dec. 13th of the last year, in which replying to another of Nov. 3rd by the Secretary of State, he informs him of some indulgences and privileges granted by the Apostolic See to Dr. Pedro Campos, secular priest, and to Father Bartolome Casanova of the St. Augustine Order, who accompanied the Catholic families of Minorca in the year 1768 selected by the English for their colony in Florida in America. He has also seen another letter from the Rev. Bishop of Minorca of the 5th of February last, who informs him that by Royal Cedula of November 7th of the past year, he has been asked regarding the manner practised in the selection of the families of Minorca and the circumstances of said prelates; he gives all the information he knows and can at present, promising that immediately upon receipt of news he expects and has asked for he will forward. Lastly that he has investigated and informed himself of the Royal order of the 1st of the present March by which these letters have passed to the Council, that they may agree in the provisions they deem worthy and advisable. For the better understanding of all this affair it must be remembered that the Governor of Havana, Don Antonio Bucareli, gave an account on the 11th of January of the referred to year, of the arrival of another certificate of the virtues of one for Beatification, directed to the Rev. Bishop and seemingly written by Dr. Pedro Campos who calls himself Parish Priest of the families of Minorca who were selected by the English for their colony of Florida; that this letter had been put in the hands of the Diocesan Prelate; that one and the other had notified his Majesty of the difficulties surrounding the request and proposition of Dr. Campos, as has been demonstrated by the antecedent documents. It is also worthy of consideration that Dr. Campos in his letter at the same time that he states the selection and transmigration of the Minorcans to Florida participates that he had been elected Parish Priest of said families, and Father Casanova, Vicar of them, which jurisdiction they had received from the Supreme Pontificate who ignored to which Bishop they were subject in that English colony; but placing them under obligation to appear by writing before the expiration of three years to the Holy See and the Diocesan Prelate that one and the other were natives of Minorca, subject under the temporal power to Great Britain and spiritually to the Bishop of Minorca, both having exercised for many years the position of priests in preaching the Gospel and moral doctrines. And for this reason they begged the Rev. Bishop of Cuba to send them patents of Parish Priest and Vicar for Father Casanova, as also the Holy Oil for baptism and extreme unction, and two assistant priests, proceeding with circumspection and secrecy and taking advantage of the fishermen of that coast, being all the inducement required for the help and benefit of the spiritual good of the Catholics. The Rev. Bishop of Cuba, considering the grave importance of the matter, refrained from replying to Dr. Campos, being ignorant of the quality and jurisdiction of his authority, and not to expose to irreverence the sacred matter of the Holy Oil, sending it to a Protestant Colony, and not knowing the person nor authority he had for exercising the place of Parish Priest, especially as the letter had not come in a legitimate way; but by the uncertain conduct of fishermen entrusted with the secret of an affair which did not seem to require this means, as there was liberty of religion observed in the English Colony, and as the Minorcans reserved the right to practise the Catholic religion.

The Judge, in view of all this, adopts the idea of the Rev. Bishop of Cuba, and approves his prudent resolution, and was of the opinion that this matter be illustrated by investigation, as to whether it was true that this authority was granted by the Apostolic See, to the Prelates Campos and Casanova—and under what terms and considerations. What subjects they were, if they had been appointed by the Diocesan of Minorca, if they were of good habits, and if the Minorcans were Catholics. If under these terms they had come to Florida with the view of carrying out the necessary orders of the Prelate and Governor of Minorca, and the Minister of your Majesty in the Court of Rome. All of which was accomplished, this being the antecedent which gives motive to the reply of the letters which have remained so long unanswered. The Minister of Rome gives information that in the month of June of 1768 were deputised as Apostolic missionaries for the English Province of Florida, the aforementioned Dr. Campos and Father Casanovas, this last as Vicar for the Minorcan families who asked of the Apostolic See, that different authority should be granted these Prelates for the term of three years, and in the meantime permission of his Holiness, according to terms which result by a simple copy which will accompany their letter. This Minister adds to have stated to his Holiness that if it were agreeable to His Majesty that this authority be promulgated and privileges granted that his only object was to please and serve the Catholic King.

The Apostolic indulgences being examined, it results that they were reduced to six: administering the sacraments, asking permission of the Bishop, and under the same condition the authority in all hidden cases of granting dispensation to the poor, for con-

tracting matrimony, to erect churches and chapels—
all these must be exercised without pay for the term
of three years, in the meantime with the approbation
of the Apostolic See. The Rev. Bishop of Minorca
says: that he cannot furnish the information asked
of him until he obtains news of his Vicar-General of
Minorca, who has not been able to execute it by writing, but he assures us that these Prelates and all the
Minorcan families were Catholics and passed to Florida carrying with them two Ecclesiastics who might be
the said Campos and Casanova. The Judge, with
reference to all, considers that he has discovered sufficient truth to assuage the just fears of the Rev. Bishop
of Cuba, to the recourse to the Apostolic See, by the
Minorcan families or of the Prelates Campos and Casanovas and the authority granted to these by his Holiness. The application for help of Dr. Campos dispels
all doubt which might arise from the distance between
Florida and the Island of Cuba. From all this results
other useful things, since all this authority granted
Dr. Campos and Father Casanovas is left at the disposal of the Bishop of Cuba and as this Prelate and to
all those of America so many pontifical authorities are
granted, he can very well make use of it for the spiritual government of the little flock of Catholics residing
in the English Colony and examine the privileges
granted to these Presbyters, adopting them according
to the nature and delegate of the authority of their
Pastoral Office. It is true that the secrecy asked by Dr.
Campos caused some misgivings, but in view of what
it expounded by the Rev. Bishop of Minorca the mystery is solved, as perhaps it has happened in Florida
as in Minorca and Minorca in regard to the disturb-

Old St. Augustine

ances of the Catholic religion, the English having been wanting in their promises drawn up in their agreement. So that, as the Vicar-General of Minorca had no expedient in his jurisdiction, the same may have happened to Dr. Campos and Father Casanovas who, in consequence of the determination of the Court of London, cannot proceed in all concerning the education and spiritual care of the Catholics.

Under these considerations the Judge feels that the Rev. Bishop of Cuba should send him a copy of all that he wishes, sharing with him the care of the faithful of Florida, governing them by means of the aforementioned ministers and taking as much forethought as his zeal dictates and he considers convenient to a good government and conversion of that Catholic portion, availing themselves of the necessary form of Governor of Havana and Captain-General of that Island of Cuba, not only for having been the means of which Dr. Campos availed himself, but also that he may communicate with the Governor and Chief of Florida, and that the Rev. Bishop of Minorca send him notice of his letter and beg him to take charge and investigate such reports as may come up, informing himself through the Vicar-General of Minorca and also of those Catholic subjects who from said Island have passed to the city of Alzuvia as we are assured in his letter. That the Commandant of Minorca be stimulated anew to obtain the information demanded of him. And that he send documents to the Marquez of Gremaldin to the effect that he send notice to the Council of the church service, which by the Secretary in charge has been made in the Courts of London at the instance of the clergy and Bishop of Minorca, and of the resolution taken by the Council, provided by the King of Great Britain. These documents being necessary, to send a copy to the Governor and Bishop of Cuba that they may proceed securely and provide such resources as are needed, for all of which they can free themselves with necessary speed. Notwithstanding the Council will remember what is most agreeable.

Madrid, April 16th, 1771.

FOR THE COUNCIL.

My Dear Sir: A. D. 1771.

I have not forgotten your Excellency's letter of Oct. 20th of 1768, in which you state to me your merits and occupation as also that of Father Bartolome Casanovas of the St. Augustine Order, and you expound to me the motives which induce you to apply to me for your title of Parish Priest of the Catholic families of Minorcans established in Mosquito, English territory of Florida, and that of Vicar for the other Priest. Also asking for the Sacred Oils with which to administer baptism and extreme unction, and for two assistant Priests of the Divine office. In order that I might reply to your claims I considered it advisable to submit it to the higher authority and intelligence of the King, my Lord, and that I might be enlightened by his Sovereign order regarding all requirements for so delicate and serious a subject. I have received all the light on the subject I wished through a Royal Cedula of Aug. 16th of the present year, composed of documents which legitimatize the character of your executive and that of your companion. The power and authority invested in you by the Holy See and the professed Catholicism of the Minorcan families to whom you both administer. Also the various instructions all relative to my government in that Catholic Colony whose obedience and prompt attention to the kind intentions of the King our Sovereign, I extend to you (by means of a safe and trusty guide) the title of Parish Priest and Vicar. A copy containing the only and extraordinary powers of the Apostolic Chair, which I hold and which I convey to your Excellency and by your death, sickness or other legitimate impediment, to your companion. That the time with the requirements expressed therein, two assistant priests of the Divine office and a box with three flasks of sacred oil, distinguished as the Chrisma, Catecuma, and for the sick. I hope soon to send you a more extended prorogation of other powers, that you may make good use of them to the benefit of that small flock, and in case of you and your companion's death, the Priest I should nominate. This is a grace that the Catholic and clement heart of the King has solicited from the Court of Rome, through the means of his Minister. It is also reserved that I shall be promptly advised of the results of the Offices made in the court of London, by order or representation of the Illustrious Bishop of Minorca, and the resolutions taken by the private council of the King of Great Britain in the month of June of the past year, with the only desire that their people do not become discouraged in the Holy Religion they profess, and that they owe such great blessings to the best of Monarchs whose large soul guides all his thoughts and intentions to the sustenance and propagation of the true Roman Faith, making it noticed and perceived by the whole world his pious and eminent care for humanity and his heroic and glorious zeal. Your Excellency will make it understood by those chosen few, the gratitude and acknowledgment these sublime demonstrations bind them to fulfill. Apply yourself to guide them and make them patient with all love and charity. Apply yourself to all this and count on my assistance in all that is needed to secure this important work. That I may better form an idea of your wants and desires to relieve them with the spiritual aid that your condition requires, it would be well you should send me immediately an individual report of the constitution, material and formula of your church and a list of the families who compose your congregation. State all excesses, and anything you deem worthy of my consideration and within my Province. These last will always have for their object the salvation of the souls confided to the good conscience and care of your Excellency and your companion, whose good conduct I flatter myself leaves nothing to desire, being perfect and complete in the discharge of his respective ministerial duties to the honor and glory of God. These are of such interest that we are obliged to sacrifice our best efforts, the repose and even loss of our own lives. I remain with best wishes and always ready to conciliate your wishes. May God guide you for many happy years.

I kiss your hand and am your affectionate and sincere Chaplain, THE BISHOP OF CUBA.

Senor Dr. Don Pedro Campos (absent).

Rev. Father Bartolome Casanova.

It agrees with the original letter and its contents, which remain in the Secretary under my charge and which I remit by order of the Bishop, my Lord. I took this out in Havana on the 3rd day of December, 1771. DR. JOSE DE LA BANDERA, Secretary.

CHAPTER XX.

A. D. 1773.

Proceedings of the Council upon information obtained from his Majesty's Minister at the Court of Rome concerning the appeal made by the Parish Priest and Vicar of the Catholic families established in the English territory of Florida—The matter contained in the different Bishops' letters, also the letters of the Priest and Vicar asking for patent and further privileges rehearsed—A report of the condition of the said Minorcan families who are dissatisfied with the lack of spiritual comforts— Have built a brick church and are very devout— Of their desire to throw off the yoke of Great Britain and their love for Spain—Reply of the Judge—Testimony sent by the Bishop of Cuba.

COUNCIL.

Report relative to information obtained from His Majesty's minister at the Court of Rome in reply to the order expedited as a result of the appeal made by the Parish Priest and Vicar of the Catholic families established in the English territory of Florida, to the Bishop of Cuba, asking for the Holy Oil.

PROCEEDINGS.

First—In Council on September 27th of last year, it was called to your Royal attention in Council, what had been represented by the Governor of Havana

Old St. Augustine 215

and Rev. Bishop of Cuba, concerning the appeal made to the Bishop of Cuba by Dr. Pedro Campos and Padre Bartolome Casanovas, the first Parish Priest, the second Vicar of the Catholic families who were taken from Minorca to colonize the territory of Florida, belonging to the English, asking for the Holy Oil, with which to administer baptism. It seemed that your Majesty's Minister in the Court of Rome was the most worthy person to solicit and obtain with promptness the information as to whether the Catholics taken from the Island of Minorca by the English in the year 1768, had made an appeal to the Holy See that they might carry with them their own Pastors, and if his Holiness had named in the capacity of Parish or Parochial Priest and Vicar of the referred to people, the Presbyters Dr. Campos and Padre Bartolome Casanovas, and what jurisdiction had been conceded to them, giving all information with the greatest clearness; also, that the correspondence and letter be expedited to the Captain-General of the Island of Minorca and the Bishop of that Diocese that they should inform separately all details they knew of the extraction of the families of Minorca made by the English to colonize Florida, if said families were Catholics and lived and behaved as such. If they went over with the privilege of the free use of their religion, and if Dr. Campos and Padre Casanovas were elected Parish Priest and Vicar of them. What was the character of these two Subjects, and if for the acceptance of this charge they gave notice and obtained permission from that Minister. In the meantime, while such steps are being taken, that they should acknowledge to the Governor of Havana and Bishop of Cuba, the receipt of their letters stating it to have been to the Royal approval of your Majesty the determination they had agreed upon—notifying each that your Majesty would take some action in the matter, but that the Bishop should try to inform himself of the manner of practising the Catholic religion by these Minorcans in Florida, and the manner of assistance by the Parish Priest and Vicar of the Catholic Town and that the same be forwarded to the Governor, so that one and the other advance the information resulting therefrom. And your Majesty having agreed in this opinion should order the corresponding Royal Cedulas and letters agreed upon with date of October 27th and November 7th of last year.

FINAL CONDITION.

In this condition the Council received a letter from the Rev. Bishop of Minorca of February 5th of this year, stating that he could not take the required steps for obtaining information asked, as he awaited news of his Vicar-General of Minorca, who had sent him some messages by word of mouth, not being able to do so by writing on account of the interference of the Governor of that Island. Notwithstanding the difficulties the Vicar had communicated to him the fact that all the families were Catholics who went to Florida with the free use of their religion, carrying with them, to serve as Parish Priest and Vicar, two Ecclesiastics, one secular and one monastic (belonging to an order), and they might be the ones mentioned. This Prelate adding that the first was a good and laborious Priest, applying himself strictly to his Ministerial duties, and had been Vicar for many years on that

Island. That of the other he did not have such good reports, although those he had were not so bad. That it was reported the English had assassinated this Priest without stating a reason for doing so. That last June, on account of the troubles between this Court and the Court of London, a decree was obtained from the private Council of the King of Great Britain that in Minorca there should be no further interference with the Ecclesiastics; that now a more quiet state exists and things are restored to their normal state, therefore the Rev. Bishop awaited news of the matter from his Vicar, having asked for it last October 27th.

Prior to this Fray Julian Ariaga had sent a document, dated March 1st of the present year, written upon the resolution of your Majesty, expressed in a letter notifying your Minister at the Court of Rome, who having verified and accomplished the same the accompanying note, showing the powers and privileges invested in Dr. Campos and Padre Casanovas. These documents are sent by order of his Majesty to the Council, that upon seeing them they may agree upon the provisions most expedient. In this letter the Minister of your Majesty in Rome states that in the month of June of 1768 they were empowered as Apostolic Missionaries for the English Province of Florida. The Minorcan families had petitioned the Holy See to invest these Prelates with certain powers, which was done, granting them these powers for a term of three years, in the meantime a Permit of His Holiness accompanied it set forth in these terms, as shown by the copy—if it should be agreeable to your Majesty that they make use of these powers and privileges—that he was only too glad and willing to serve and please so good and Catholic a King.

From the above mentioned letter of indulgences, it appears that they are six, reduced to the administering of the Parochial Sacraments, obtaining first permission from the Bishop or his Vicar. These places are near, not further than two days' journey of ten leagues each day by land from the Province of Florida, and under the same conditions these Priests are invested with the power of absolving abroad all such hidden cases, although it be reserved for the Holy See to give dispensation to the poor, where they wish to contract matrimony within certain degrees of kinship. Some of these privileges of dispensation are granted to some Priests approved by their Bishop. They could construct churches and chapels in the Colony under the same restrictions of getting a permit from the Diocesan Bishop, if not absent and at too great a distance. These privileges were to be exercised in a gracious manner for only three years, in the meantime under permit of the Holy See. The Council of March 4th of this year, having agreed that this expedient be transferred to the Judge with the former proceedings. In his reply of August 16th is the following. With regard to all that is stated he says: that he discovers ample reasons to quiet the mind and anxieties indicated by the Bishop of Cuba, as it is evident the Minorcan families obtain direct permission from the Holy See granting these powers to Dr. Campos and Padre Casanovas—leaving them, however, subordinates to the Diocesan Bishop while he was not at too great a distance. That the proceedings of Dr. Campos remove all doubt which might arise

Old St. Augustine 219

of the distance of the Bishop, as this Presbyter recognizes him as his own and proper Pastor. From this the Judge decides that the Bishop of Cuba can grant, without any further fear, the requests of Dr. Campos; that he should contribute to it, not alone for the consolation it would bring those Catholic families, but also to confirm and establish his jurisdiction, and have it under his control in all things concerning the Faith. Under these terms occur many others which are useful, as the privileges are granted these Ecclesiastics, but places them legally under control of the Bishop of Cuba. And as to this Prelate, as well as to all those in America, such ample privileges are granted, he might well avail himself of them for the spiritual government of the flock of Catholics residing in the English Colony. He could examine the privileges conceded and interpret them as the new ones of his Pastoral Office. It is true that the caution and secrecy used by Dr. Campos caused some anxiety and suspicion, but in view of what the Rev. Bishop of Minorca says, the mystery is discovered, supposing that the same circumstances had arisen in Florida as in Minorca, and there had been religious disturbances, or that the English had failed to comply with the treaties of the capitulation. That as the Vicar-General of Minorca was prevented from carrying on his correspondence with the Diocese of Minorca, the same might have occurred with Dr. Campos, owing to the proceedings at the Court of London he could have no intercourse with any other Diocese. That aside from these considerations, which are to be regretted, the Judge considers it well for the Bishop of Cuba to retain a copy with all the particulars given by the

Bishop of Minorca, referring to the good standing of the Catholics who emigrated to the English Colony, and that the high standing of Dr. Campos and Padre Casanovas and send a literal copy of the privileges granted to them by the Apostolic See, omitting the expression used in the summary of the "Bula de la Cena." But that the Bishop make use of all the privileges granted him, and expedite the titles of Parochial Pastor and Vicar which have been asked of him in such terms as are best suited for the present, and send them the Holy Oils, if nothing new should arise to prevent it. So care for the faithful of Florida and govern them by means of these same Ministers—using all the zeal and care he considers good for them —making use of the Governor of Havana and the Captain-General if necessary. Not only that he was the means used by Dr. Campos for obtaining these concessions, but that documents may be passed between himself and the Governor of Florida, he should have the Bishop of Minorca to acknowledge receipt of his letter, and beg him to verify the reports and information given by the Vicar-General of Minorca of those Catholic subjects who passed from the City of Alusia (Alcubea) as he assures us in his letter. That the commandant of Minorca make it obligatory that he give this information asked, and that an official report be made of it and sent to the Marquis of Grimaldi that he in turn may report it to the Council as his individual report of what the secretary under his charge has done in the Court of London at the representation of the Clergy and Bishop of Minorca and the resolution taken by the private Council of the King of Great Britain in the month of June of the past year,

Old St. Augustine 221

as affirmed by the same Bishop. These documents are necessary according as what may be produced or forwarded by the Governor or Bishop of Cuba, so as to proceed with security and remit to the Ministers of Florida the necessary resources and forward categorical documents if found necessary. By means of these dispatches and letters all things may be facilitated.

NOTE.

This expedient being ready for the Councils, two letters have been received, one from the proclaimed Bishop of Minorca and the other from the Commandant of that Island, Marques de Alos, both dated April 22nd of the present year. The first states that in consequence of what he spoke of in his preceding letter of February 5th, that an account of the troubles on the Island of Minorca in trying to open war with this Court, His Vicar-General who resides there did not dare to answer His letter of December 14th past, regarding the various families who had passed into Florida. That only by a note, without his signature, did he intimate that this Priest had the title of Prelate and the power to confess and preach. That he was a person of merit, capacity and virtue. That the Monk who accompanied him had the license and power to preach and hear confessions; that immediately after the publication of peace he heard from the same Vicar, who after writing of several affairs corresponding to his ministerial duties, He states that from his Parish alone on account of the great suffering from failures of crops, there had gone to Florida with others from that Island and Spain, more than three hundred families. They were urged by insinuations from the Government who offered them homes, with land to cultivate and hold and the free use of their Catholic religion, adding these remarks regarding the proclaimed Priests: Dr. Campos, who had served as Vicar and Parish Priest in the Parish of Mercadal, had asked him for letters and testimonials to pass over to Florida, which he granted and in them stated the good character He bore and exemplary life He had led and good work he had done for the Church, having served many years as Vicar and being well versed in literature. The St. Augustine Monk who accompanied Him was Padre Bartolome Casanovas; he found nothing wrong in His conduct; He had preached in the Parish of Alazor and was consequently the Confessor of men; he did not remember more. He concludes his letter stating that this is about all He can say on the subject. The Commandant, Marques de Alos, in His letter stated that He had not been able sooner to make the necessary inquiries and comply with the order on account of the differences between this Court and that of London, but that things having quieted he has been able to ascertain that the transmigration of these families was made by the offer of lands to cultivate and retain with the free use of their Catholic Religion as practised by the Minorcans of that Island, according to the treaty between both Courts. That Dr. Campos was assistant Parish Priest of Mercadal—a Priest of exemplary life and habits, taking with Him his credentials from the Vicar of the Diocese in Mahon. It was supposed that the Augustine Monk went also with permission of his Superior, but of that nothing certain was obtained, as that portion of the Island of Minorca was under the dominion of Great Britain,

Old St. Augustine 223

and only the Ecclesiastics recognized the superiority of the Bishop of that Diocese—this was all he could certify in obedience to the command received. Later a letter came from the Bishop of Cuba, dated February 19th; on the same subject in response to the order sent by Royal Cedula of November 7th, he says: That having devoted himself to find out, with every precaution, he was able to obtain the following information from one of the fishermen who has been in the Catholic Minorcan settlement. That these families are established in their homes, the house of Dr. Campos and Padre Casanovas being the principal one of the place. They have a church built of brick, quite commodious and decent; that having obtained last year large and abundant crops of corn and indigo, they loaded two vessels with indigo, but that they are dissatisfied on account of the number of deaths occurring among them and also the lack of spiritual comforts from this same Priest, who had asked for the Holy Oil of the Bishop of Cuba. That most of the Minorcan Colonists are very devout; He saw them daily praying the Rosary and receiving communion, but all wish to throw off the yoke of Great Britain and pass again to the dominion of your Majesty—demonstrating with strong and lively expressions their love and conservatism for the Crown of Spain. This I believe, from all He tells me, He saw during His stay among them. The Bishop concludes by stating: It is all he can tell us regarding this affair, but he has taken steps for further information which he will forward to your Majesty when obtained. All of which I make known to the Council that it may proceed as most convenient.

Number 87—3—27— Year 1773.

REPLY OF THE JUDGE.

The Judge being cognizant of your Majesty's Royal Decree regarding the consultation held by the Government on December 10th, 1772, at which time said Tribunal recalling the proceedings and last state of the expedient of the Minorcan families who passed over to Florida, with the free use of their Catholic religion, he brings to the consideration of your Majesty, among other things, that they implore of the Apostolic See the grace and power for the actual missionaries of the Commission or Bull from the Vatican, that they may administer the Sacrament of confirmation to these faithful ones, while the Bishop of Cuba does not dare concede these powers to them, on account of the natives and his peculiar Episcopal dignity. That your Royal person deign to confer with the Council in the following terms. As the Judge has decided, it seems proper that my Minister in Rome should supplicate the Vatican for a Bull, granting power to these missionaries, and have it sent by the reserved way for their direction. In obedience to this sovereign resolution, and to accomplish it in the spirit intended, the Judge has had present the origin of this affair and the motive which actuated the sentiment of the Council to the referred consultation of December 10th, and with reference to one and the other He has found the minutes which are rubricated by His hand, and accompany this reply. The proclaimed minutes comprehend a general idea of the manner and style in which the Minister of this Court in Rome should present the supplication and urge the granting thereof in the order and regularity with which these affairs are conducted in the Offices and Tribunals of

Rome. The Judge has not seen proper to state the form of these Bulls, leaving that to the arbitration of your Majesty's Minister, that time may not be lost when the opportunity presents itself. The Judge feels that if the Council finds nothing to correct in the minutes they should be sent by the "via reservada" as arranged by the Royal Decree already mentioned, that your Majesty may give it the direction which corresponds and is of your Royal pleasure.

Madrid, Aug. 21st, 1773.

TESTIMONY SENT BY THE BISHOP OF CUBA.

Sire:

With regard to the Royal Cedula of the present January 3rd in which your Royal Highness advises me to assist, care for, and aid the Catholic Minorcan families established in the English Territory of Florida, in accord with the Governor of the Post, I have given the interlocutory decree comprehended in the testimony which I remit to your Majesty for your sovereign approval.

May God preserve your Majesty for many years.

SANTIAGO JOSE, Bishop of Cuba.

Havana, June 30th, 1773.

CHAPTER XXI.

A. D. 1773-1786.

Letter from the King to the Bishop of Cuba concerning the petition soliciting an extension of time and the privileges conceded to Dr. Pedro Campos and Padre Bartolome Casanovas, Parochial Priest and Vicar of Catholic families of Minorca in Florida—Enclosing an open mandate of his Holiness enlarging and extending the time for twenty years, Madrid, 1773—A copy of a letter and statement sent in by Lieutenant of Hibernians, Don Nicholas Grenier, in regard to the importance of the St. Johns and St. Marys river Provinces, stating the need to his Majesty of vessels armed to impress and control these Provinces which are rich in timber, turpentine, pitch and tar—Considers it detrimental to Spanish interests for Americans to introduce any commerce in those Provinces—Letter for the Captain-General of Florida to the Governor of the post of St. Augustine concerning the great necessity of further protecting the Spanish interests along the St. Marys and St. Johns rivers—Tranquility of the country jeopardized by outlaws—Some have been arrested and paid the penalty with their lives—Matter referred to the Governor, 1774.

THE KING TO THE REV. FATHER IN CHRIST, BISHOP OF THE HOLY CHURCH, CATHEDRAL OF SANTIAGO DE CUBA.

In a letter of August 29th, 1771, I am informed by Don Lamas Acpuro, Archbishop, who was of Valencia and my Minister to the Court of Rome, that in virtue of a warning from the Marquez of Grimalde in a letter of July 23rd, he had formed the corresponding petition soliciting an extension of time of the privileges conceded to Dr. Pedro Campos and Padre Bartolome Casanovas, Parochial Priest and Vicar of the Catholic families of Minorca, who went to establish themselves in the English territory of Florida, asking also that his Holiness accord to these Ecclesiastics and their successors the other graces and privileges needed to administer to the spiritual nourishment of their flocks—and having deemed it desirable to transmit them through Monsenor Zelada of whom they had also availed themselves to investigate the truth of these privileges, being one of the Prelates who served in the Tribunal of the Holy Office. He immediately complied with the petition in consequence of having sent it to his Holiness at the instigation of Monsenor Antonelli, assistant of the same Tribunal, who spoke to his Holiness in audience, using his favorable influence with the result shown in his letter to Monsenor Zelada of August 24th, informing him that his Holiness extended these privileges to twenty years—asking if he had complied with the balance of the communication for greater privileges and followed the instructions mentioned in the open mandate. He replied asking if he would pass on to solicit in the practical way which was proper, and hoping it would deserve my approbation. Having seen the referred to document with my Council of the Indias, represented by Marquis de la Torre, Governor and Captain-General of that Island, by letter dated December 4th, 1771, concerning what you had done in consequence of the warning given you in the affair of the aforementioned families, explained by my Judge, and consulted me regarding it about the last of December past. I have resolved (among other things) to send the aforementioned open Mandate which has been obtained from his Holiness to certify to you the enlargement and extension of time granted the aforesaid Dr. Campos and Padre Casanovas and charging you (as I do) to use all means that are proper for your Pastoral Ministry and those of his Holiness, it has latterly been conceded you—having present by Chapter 28 of the Mandate, you can communicate it to all the Priests whom it may effect, and as the notice given you by the referred to Royal Cedula of August 16th, 1771, you will attend to and aid spiritually all the Catholics of Florida, this being my will. THE KING.

Madrid, August 4th, 1773.

Excellent Sire:

I enclose you a copy of a letter and statement which by my order was sent in by Lieutenant of Hibernians Don Nicholas Grenier, upon his return from the River St. Mary's where since my arrival I have placed him rather as a Commissioned than a detached Officer, as I have before notified your Majesty, because it has seemed to me that is the most important place in this Province as no doubt it will be in the future, on account of its fine and accessible Bar, the abundance of magnificent timber, the thorough knowledge the English have of the river, the scarcity of this nation for building material would be a stimulus to the Bahamas as well as to Satavento and Barlovento, that in future they should be supplied from them. In a previous report I stated to your Majesty the necessity I felt for two vessels for said river and the St. John's, but today I consider it my duty to make known to your Majesty the great need we have of vessels, and would ask that you send a Man-of-war with some schooners, launches and boats around as reserve guards, not only for the St. Mary's, but the St. John's also, where the Bar, although not as many feet deep as the St. Mary's, is better and its waters are navigable for larger vessels thirty leagues up the river, and its banks abound in magnificent timber, especially the pine, from which the English have taken many millions of barrels of turpentine, pitch and tar. I also consider it important to have the armed vessels to secure the tranquility of this Country and put a restraint upon the many disturbers of peace who not knowing where to go and wishing to remain in the Province refused to be subjected to Government or laws of any kind. It is certain that in such cases a few armed vessels would make more impression than two regiments since the swamps and woods make it almost impossible for them to operate. The twenty-five Dragoons I now have are not sufficient to maintain my orders with the proper authority, therefore I fear to issue orders not to compromise the dignity of this Government. My only resource and hope is that your Majesty will place me in a position where, when occasion demands, I can act with the proper spirit and decorum. God preserve you for many years.

St. Augustine, November 12th, 1784.

The Unwritten History of

COPY OF LETTER OF COMMANDANT OF DETACHED BODY OF TROOPS
ON THE ST. MARYS RIVER TO THE GOVERNOR OF FLORIDA.

My Dear Sir:

Acting upon the order imposed upon me by His Majesty, when I presented myself for resignation of the commission under my charge on the river St. Mary's. I enclose adjusted a report stating as far as my ability allows all that I have observed and consider worthy of your notice. God preserve you many years. NICOLAS GRENIER.

STATEMENT.

The Bar of St. Mary's, so called, although its true name is Bar of Amelia, is considered one of the best and least dangerous of the America Septentional. Vessels of 500 tons can enter. On either side are Islands. The one on the right is called Cumberland, belonging to the Americans; it is sparsely inhabited, exceedingly fertile in timber, as American vessels come to cut it. The one on the left is called Amelia, its land is considered very fertile, producing pine, cedar and oak in abundance. Its inhabitants number some twenty families; these people belong as much to one Island as the other, being variable and erratic in their habits. The distance between Amelia and Cumberland, which forms the channel where all vessels going up the St. Mary's are obliged to pass, is more or less—miles. For this reason a Fort or Castle at the northern extremity of Amelia would be of the greatest advantage. The channel formed by these Islands is at the mouth of the river. In front of these Islands is a third one called Tiger, entirely depopulated, as it is sterile, full of swamps and lakes so that

Old St. Augustine 231

no advantage can be derived from it. From the anchoring grounds of Amelia to the entrance of St. Mary's river is a distance of one and a half miles and the River is navigable for forty miles. At the mouth of said River there is a place called by the English New Town or Princetown which was selected for building a City, but the work was never carried out. The number of outlaws between the towns of St. John's and St. Mary's is about sixty families. Among them some might be useful to our Nation, but the others the sooner we drive them out of the Province the better, as they are men who have neither God nor law, and men who are capable of the greatest atrocities. There is another River further in where vessels can navigate for several miles, but it requires an experienced pilot, on account of the numerous sand banks and small streams and the most experienced are frequently deceived. There are four or five other small Islands. The Talbot, St. George, Doctor and the Pierce, all these Islands, although in themselves small, are of much value for their beautiful pines, cedars and oaks. I consider it detrimental to our interests that the Americans introduce any commerce in this Province, and at the same time I believe the best way to prevent it would be to establish a fleet. These Islands produce timber to build the vessels.

NICOLAS GRENIER.

St. Augustine, Fla., Nov. 10th, 1784.

1786.
LETTER FOR THE CAPTAIN-GENERAL OF FLORIDA TO THE GOVERNOR OF THE POST OF ST. AUGUSTINE.

Don Vicente Manuel de Cespedes gave an account in three letters directed to your Excellency that Don

Nicolas Grenier, who commanded the detached company on the River St. Mary's, stated the urgency and necessity of protecting that post for the advantages which would accrue from it to the Royal service, and tranquility of the Country. The inhabitants have openly declared against us, but conceal themselves in wilderness on the banks of the St. John's as far as St. Mary's controlling that Province. He warned the English Governor Don Patrick Louin to prosecute the perfidity of such men, if he would secure a peaceful Government. The opinion he had formed of them was afterwards confirmed by the frequent thefts and deprivation, it could not be remedied for the want of aid. Under such circumstances I judge it better to wait and allow them to leave and then vigorously oppose their re-entering the Province. At present, the beginning of the year 1785, we find ourselves free from many of the principal leaders of them, who went over to Pensacola and other English settlements and to the United States, where some have paid the penalty of their misdeeds with their lives. The Senor Louin seemed to think the time had arrived when they should be prosecuted, and so he sent to arrest one of the outlaws, Daniel Mc————, in the name of Great Britain. Candido Salteador and Guillermo Cunningham are even worse than the others, being constant receivers of stolen goods. He afterwards gave them their liberty under bond that they should leave the Province with the tide, using the launch San Pedro to convey them, he made them take oath never to re-enter the Province nor surrounding country. We are to consult with Providence as to what steps must be taken with Cunningham's wife and children. The reports having

Old St. Augustine 233

been examined by the Council of Indians, they have decided to take no steps at present, the King agreeing to the proposition, and his Majesty commands me to return your Excellency the above referred reports and testimonials, that as Captain-General of the Province of St. Augustine, is to proceed in the case, as your Excellency, under the circumstances, should determine in things of weight as well as in minor affairs, as behooves a Governor of Florida. Render a just account of the results, and of the Royal Order. I warn your Excellency that you fulfill it.

God preserve you for many years.

SENOR.

Madrid, December 5th, 1786.

www.ingramcontent.com/pod-product-compliance
Lightning Source LLC
Chambersburg PA
CBHW070547050426
42450CB00011B/2760